Bible
Oases

*Spiritual
Refreshment From
Unlikely Places*

Ivor Powell

Books by Ivor Powell

Bible Oases

Spiritual Refreshment From Unlikely Places

Ivor Powell

kregel
PUBLICATIONS

Grand Rapids, MI 49501

Bible Oases: Spiritual Refreshment From Unlikely Places by Ivor Powell.

Copyright © 1994 by Ivor Powell.

Published in 1994 by Kregel Publications, a division of Kregel, Inc., P.O. Box 2607, Grand Rapids, MI 49501. Kregel Publications provides trusted, biblical publications for Christian growth and service. Your comments and suggestions are valued.

Cover Photograph: Patricia Sgrignoli, POSITIVE IMAGES
Cover Design: Alan G. Hartman

Library of Congress Cataloging-in-Publication Data
Powell, Ivor, 1910-
    Bible Oases: spiritual refreshment from unlikely places / Ivor Powell.
        p.   cm.
    Includes index.
    1. God—Promises—Biblical teaching. I. Title.
BS491.5.P69   1994   242'.5—dc20   94-17880
                                                                                CIP
ISBN 0-8254-3520-x (paperback)

1 2 3 4 5 Printing / Year 98 97 96 95 94

Printed in the United States of America

CONTENTS

SECTION ONE
The Old Testament

SECTION TWO
The Great Physician Who Made House Calls

SECTION THREE
The New Testament

Many years ago I was urged by my teachers to study the Bible, but when I began to search the Scriptures, I discovered some parts of the sacred writings were more attractive than others. I did not appreciate the long lists of names and frequently looked elsewhere in search of something more attractive. Many Christians read the Psalms of David, the four Gospels, and the Acts of the Apostles but neglect portions of the Old Testament because the material appears to be a wilderness in which spiritual refreshment is difficult to find.

I am grateful that I learned to explore the less-popular portions of the Bible, for I discovered that in the most unlikely places was truth which made an indelible impression upon my mind. At the close of one of my meetings a delightful lady asked, "Now why didn't I see that before? I have read that verse hundreds of times, but I must have been blind." I knew what she meant! The Bible is a remarkable volume containing treasure of incalculable worth. The title of this book expresses that fact. A desert is not always an attractive place unless one happens to be a collector of plants which thrive in those inhospitable regions.

To reach an oasis with its palm trees, shade, and life-sustaining water is an unforgettable experience. It suggests that even the Creator knew where people would need assistance urgently. Perhaps the Scriptures resemble a country. There are tall hills where the scenery is entrancing and beautiful meadows where flowers bloom and bees make honey. Gold is seldom found in areas famous for agriculture. The world's greatest oil deposits exist in deserts or localities hard to reach. Explorers have been rewarded because their persistent search took them into almost inaccessible parts of the world. I appreciate the "hard to understand" verses in the Bible and have been refreshed by the living water which came from unlikely places. Over a period of years I was an ardent collector of rare sea shells. I walked along deserted beaches where only the sound of the waves and the cries of seagulls broke the silence. When I turned over the rocks I often found rare items hidden in the sand. It was magnificent training for many of God's choicest gems await discovery beneath the strangest texts. Everybody should learn how to look beneath and beyond perplexing paragraphs for by so doing souls can be enriched eternally.

I am indebted once again to Kregel Publications of Grand Rapids, Michigan. It is remarkable how my publishers can transform a manuscript into an object of beauty. With untiring patience and outstanding skill, they have helped to send my books around the world. I shall always be indebted to them.

IVOR POWELL

SECTION ONE
The Old Testament

"And the Lord appeared unto Abram, and said, Unto thy seed will I give this land: and there builded he an altar unto the Lord, who appeared unto him" (Gen. 12:7).

This text introduces two men who began a journey together. They had a common goal but unfortunately were separated from the one another. One climbed a mountain to a place where the atmosphere was clean and pure, where vision was unlimited. His companion descended into the plains of Sodom where opportunities for a successful business career appeared to be excellent. The land was productive; cattle were fat, and laughter echoed from the nearby city. Sodom was an attractive place for people who ignored pollution. Even poor folk could become rich if they were willing to destroy their souls. Abram and his nephew looked at the well-watered plains of Sodom, but increasing strife necessitated a separation of the two men. "And Lot lifted up his eyes, and beheld all the plain of Jordan, that it was well watered every where. . . . Then Lot chose him all the plain of Jordan; and Lot journeyed east; and they separated themselves the one from the other. Abram dwelled in the land of Canaan, and Lot dwelled in the cities of the plain, and pitched his tent toward Sodom" (Gen. 13:10–12).

One detail explained the difference between the two men. Abram loved to erect altars; Lot did not. Possibly he had occasionally knelt at his uncle's altar, but he never built one of his own. Abram looked toward heaven; Lot looked toward the cities of the plain. The older man was thrilled by the grace of God; his nephew was influenced by greed and ambition and became the wealthiest pauper of his generation. These men could belong to any family, church, or community and be business associates or intimate friends. Yet they might be very different from each other. The man who kneels daily at an altar cannot be far away from God. Anyone who is too busy to pray walks on a dangerous highway. Abram built four altars which represented stages of spiritual growth.

The Altar of Conversion . . . *How Wonderful—The Place of Pardon*

Abram erected his first altar in the plain of Moreh, which was the culmination of a long journey from Ur of the Chaldees. As far as is known he never had any inclination earlier to erect any altar. His father Terah worshiped idols, and it is extremely unlikely that any other religion was permitted to interfere with that practice (see Josh. 24:2). Abram would have been a loyal son, subject to the authority of his parent. Then, in some unrevealed way, God spoke to him; everything changed for the son of Terah. "Now the LORD had said unto Abram, Get thee out of thy country, and from thy kindred, and from thy father's house, unto a land that I will shew thee: And I will make of thee a great nation, and I will bless thee, and make thy name great; and thou shalt be a blessing" (Gen. 12:1–2). There is reason to believe that in the estimation of his neighbors Abram was exceptionally foolish. When he tried to explain the reason for his departure into the desert, his answers were not conclusive. He had heard a voice calling him but had no knowledge of the One who called him. He did not know where he was going or what he would do when he reached his destination. Had he become insane? Nevertheless, Abram obeyed the whisper that troubled his soul and aroused his conscience. Centuries later, wise men followed a star to find the infant Christ. Abram had no such guide; he went in faith, "for he looked for a city which hath foundations, whose builder and maker is God" (Heb. 11:10).

Terah accompanied his son on the journey from Ur and was probably a great hindrance to everybody. When he reached Haran, the center of moon worship, he decided to stay there. Many years later Abram reached Canaan. The long trek through sandy wastes was hazardous and difficult, but ultimately he reached the Promised Land and, arriving in the plains of Mamre, erected his first altar. "*And the LORD appeared unto Abram.*" While the patriarch lived in Ur of the Chaldees, *he heard a voice calling* him; when he knelt before an altar, *he met God.*

That was one of the earliest glimpses of evangelical truth. When the call of God reaches the soul of a sinner, its message is disturbing, but when a person reaches the place of sacrifice—the Cross of Calvary—God appears to the believing soul, and His presence becomes real. The poet expressed this fact when he wrote:

> At the Cross, at the Cross,
> Where I first saw the light:
> And the burden of my heart rolled away:
> It was there by faith,
> I received my sight,
> And now I am happy all the day.

11

"And he removed from thence unto a mountain on the east of Bethel, and pitched his tent, having Bethel on the west, and Hai on the east; and there *he builded an altar unto the LORD, and called upon the name of the LORD*" (Gen. 12:8). When Abram knelt at his first altar, God met with him. At his second altar he prayed, and this became a daily custom. He had lived many years without knowing the Lord; now he planned to meet Him every day. Abram enjoyed being with Jehovah. To listen to His voice was to hear the music of another world. The patriarch was always safe when he lingered near the altar of Jehovah. There was never a famine "in the land" when God and His servant were together.

"And Abram journeyed, going on still toward the south. And there was a famine in the land: And Abram went down into Egypt" (Gen. 12:9–10). During his sojourn in Egypt he never had an altar and had no fellowship with God. His faith was shattered; memories haunted his soul, and he was an unhappy man. Eventually, when his life was threatened, he regretted his mistakes and did his utmost to correct the situation. "And Abram went up out of Egypt . . . unto the place where his tent had been at the beginning, between Bethel and Hai; *Unto the place of the altar, which he had made there at the first; and there Abram called on the name of the LORD*" (Gen. 13:1–4).

It is always wise to pray, but it is particularly important to do so when guilt harasses the soul. It is written that on both occasions when Abram visited the altar at Bethel, *he called upon the name of the Lord, and his problems were solved.* A story has been told of a small child who finished her prayer saying:

"Goodbye, dear Lord. We are moving to New York. It has been nice knowing you. Amen." Had Abram been foolish he might have finished his prayer in a similar fashion when he moved from the plain of Moreh to the mountain on the east of Bethel. Instead, the patriarch could have said with David, "Whither shall I go from thy spirit? or whither shall I flee from thy presence? If I ascend up into heaven, thou art there; if I make my bed in hell, behold, thou art there. If I take the wings of the morning, and dwell in the uttermost parts of the sea; Even there shall thy hand lead me, and thy right hand shall hold me" (Ps. 139:7–10). It is wonderful to meet God at the altar, but it is better to meet Him there *every day.*

"Then Lot chose him all the plain of Jordan; and Lot journeyed east; and they separated themselves the one from the other. Abram dwelled in the land of Canaan, and Lot dwelled in the cities of the plain. . . . And the LORD said unto Abram, after that Lot was separated from him, Lift up now thine eyes, and look from the place where thou art northward, and southward, and eastward, and westward: For all the land which thou seest, to thee will I give it, and to thy seed for ever. . . . Then Abram removed his tent, and came and dwelt in the plain of Mamre, which is in Hebron, and *built there an altar unto the LORD*" (Gen. 13:11–18). It is interesting that at his third altar Abram never asked for anything—he had been given everything!

"And Abram said unto Lot, Let there be no strife, I pray thee, between me and thee, and between my herdmen and thy herdmen; for we be brethren. Is not the whole land before thee? separate thyself, I pray thee, from me: If thou wilt take the left hand, then I will go to the right; or if thou depart to the right hand, then I will go to the left" (Gen. 13:8–9). It became increasingly evident that Abram, who lived close to his God, detested strife. To the patriarch it was more desirable to enjoy peace than riches. His fellowship at the altar was spoiled by discord within his camp. Something had to be done quickly, and he never expected God to do what was his own responsibility.

There was no need to seek divine guidance, for the man who knelt at the altar was receptive to suggestions made by the Spirit of God. Tranquility within the soul is impossible when alien forces pollute the human sanctuary. Compromise with evil is never wise when a soul strives to please God. When Lot chose to seek his fortune among the people of the plains, God rewarded Abram by giving to him far more than he could have acquired even had he lived for thousands of years. It was unnecessary to seek the guidance of God when the issue was a choice between good and evil. Abram never forgot how the Lord said to him, "Arise, walk through the land in the length of it, and in the breadth of it; for I will give it unto thee. Then Abram removed his tent and came and dwelt in the plain of Mamre, which is in Hebron, *and built there an altar unto the LORD*" (Gen. 13:17–18). This was an Old Testament expression of a truth taught by the Savior, "But seek ye first the kingdom of God, and his righteousness, and all these things shall be added unto you" (Matt. 6:33).

"And they came to the place which God had told him of; *and Abram built an altar there*, and laid the wood in order, and bound Isaac his son, and laid him on the altar upon the wood" (Gen. 22:9). An interesting progression of thought is found in the four altars erected by Abram. The first was a place of *pardon*, the second of *prayer*, the third of *praise*, and the fourth of *provision*. The path of complete surrender is never smooth. Sometimes it is difficult to appreciate the wisdom of God, for His ideas are more comprehensive than ours. It was devastating when Abraham was instructed to sacrifice Isaac. What wisdom could be found in such an act? "And Abraham rose up early in the morning, and saddled his ass, and took two of his young men with him, and Isaac his son, and clave the wood for the burnt offering, and rose up, and went unto the place of which God had told him" (Gen. 22:3). During that journey the anxious father considered the promises of God and reached a thrilling conclusion. It was never safe nor wise to judge by appearances. Jehovah had promised to bless the children of Isaac, and therefore Isaac could not die childless. If the Lord permitted the boy to die, He would have to raise him from the dead or risk being called untruthful. That conclusion enabled Abram to say to his servants, "Abide ye here with the ass; and I and the lad will go yonder and worship, *and come again to thee*" (Gen. 22:5). That trusting father promised to return *with his son*, and that would have been impossible if Isaac died.

Many years later, the writer to the Hebrews said, "By faith Abraham, when he was tried, offered up Isaac: and he that had received the promises offered his only begotten son. Of whom it was said, That in Isaac shall thy seed be called: Accounting that *God was able to raise him up*, even from the dead; from whence also he received him in a figure" (Heb. 11:17–19). That inspiring belief in the faithfulness of God brought Abraham victoriously through his greatest ordeal. Had he not understood the reliability of the Almighty, it would have been difficult to obey His strange command. He believed Jehovah was too wise to make mistakes and too loving to be unkind. With unwavering faith, "Abraham stretched forth his hand, and took the knife to slay his son. And the angel of the LORD called unto him out of heaven, and said Abraham, Abraham: and he said, Here am I. And he said, Lay not thine hand upon the lad, neither do any thing unto him: for now I know that thou fearest

God, seeing thou hast not withheld thy son, thine only son from me" (Gen. 22:10–12). When the relieved father turned to see a ram caught by his horns in the nearby thicket, he knew the Lord had again demonstrated His loving kindness. Abraham lived close to his altars, and as the Psalmist said, "He that dwelleth in the secret place of the Most High shall abide under the shadow of the Almighty" (Ps. 91:1). The patriarch earned the right to be called *"The Friend of God"* (see James 2:23).

"And while he lingered, the men laid hold upon his hand, and upon the hand of his wife, and upon the hand of his two daughters; the Lord being merciful unto him: and they brought him forth, and set him without the city" (Gen. 19:16)

Lot was one of the most indecisive men mentioned in the Bible. He was seldom in a hurry and, except for one notable occasion, dragged his feet! When strife began to exist between his workers and those of Abraham, he could have tried to solve the problem—but did not. As the trouble increased, he could have sought Abram's assistance—but did not. When he became a resident of Sodom, his conscience troubled him, but he refused to leave. When the city was about to be destroyed, the angels told him to flee, but he hesitated until God's messengers enforced departure. Lot was instructed to flee to the mountain, but he argued and chose another city in which to live. He and his wife were informed not to look back, but his wife disobeyed and died. The man was always procrastinating. He believed there would be a tomorrow, so why rush today?

The Man Who Lost His Father . . . *Distressing*

"Now these are the generations of Terah: Terah begat Abram, Nahor, and Haran; and *Haran begat Lot. And Haran died before his father Terah in the land of his nativity,* in Ur of the Chaldees" (Gen. 11:27–28). The death of Haran possibly explains why the younger man became dependent upon his uncle, Abram. The ages of the two men remain unknown, but the Bible states Abram was seventy-five years of age when he left the city of Haran (see Gen. 12:4). Considering that people lived for great periods of time, he was, relatively speaking, a young man when he heard the call of God. Lot, the son of Abram's brother, would have been at least twenty to thirty years younger. His mother was never mentioned by the ancient writer, but if she were already dead, the orphaned son would instinctively welcome any affection shown by his nearest relative. The childless Abram and the parentless Lot were attracted to each other. One found a son; the other discovered fatherly affection of which he had been deprived.

Probably the young man became increasingly dependent upon Abram, and when his uncle announced his intention to leave Ur, Lot decided to accompany him. Abram supervised the affairs of his nephew and helped as the bereaved young man faced his future. Any separation at that time would have been unthinkable. "And Terah took Abram his son, and Lot the son of Haran his son's son, and Sarai his daughter-in-law, his son Abram's wife, and they went forth with them from Ur of the Chaldees, to go into the land of Canaan; and they came unto Haran, and dwelt there" (Gen. 11:31).

The fact that Lot's possessions increased tremendously suggests the association with his uncle returned excellent dividends, but, unfortunately, success inflated his ego.

The Man Who Lost His Fellowship . . . *Dangerous*

"And there was a strife between the herdmen of Abram's cattle and the herdmen of Lot's cattle. . . . And Abram said unto Lot, Let there be no strife, I pray thee, between me and thee, and between my herdmen and thy herdmen; for we be brethren" (Gen. 13:7–8). Although there is evidence the area was populated, the abundance of water in the Jordan River guaranteed adequate supplies for everybody. That the herds had been grazing in the lower parts of hills implies that competition had arisen regarding water rights and the time when the animals could drink at the wells or mountain streams. When the workmen insisted on their privileges, the camp was filled with hostility. Apparently this did not annoy Lot, for he intended to support his men at any cost. Yet Abram was grieved to see discord among brethren; he knew it was difficult to live at peace with God and be at war with relatives.

"And Abram said unto Lot. . . . Is not the whole land before thee? . . . If thou wilt take the left hand, then I will go to the right; or if thou depart to the right hand, then I will go to the left. And Lot lifted up his eyes, and beheld all the plain of Jordan, that it was well watered every where, before the LORD destroyed Sodom and Gomorrah, even as the garden of the LORD. . . . Then Lot chose him all the plain of Jordan; and Lot journeyed east: and they separated themselves the one from the other. Abram dwelled in the land of Canaan, and Lot dwelled in the cities of the plain, and pitched his tent toward Sodom" (Gen. 13:8–12).

It might be assumed that Lot would have recognized the value of Abram's presence, fellowship, and business expertise. His uncle had forgotten more than he would ever learn. If a modern definition may be used, Lot had grown too big for his britches! Success had changed him. When he looked upon the plains of Jordan, his eyes shone with pleasure as he contemplated ways to become wealthy. Unfortunately, the man never considered what might happen to his soul. Many years later the Savior spoke about a prodigal son who made a similar mistake. Despising the fellowship of his father, the son went into a far country to seek his fortune. There the boy discovered that fools and their money were soon parted. To live among pigs was a poor substitute for an armchair close to a warm fire and a father's affection. People continue to make the same mistake; they never miss the water of fellowship until the well has gone dry!

The Man Who Lost His Faithfulness . . . *Destructive*

Lot exchanged his uncle's embrace for the taunts and sneers of homosexuals. The cattle increased, but his spirituality declined. Increasing popularity became evident, for "he sat in the gate." His men toiled in the sunlit plains while he listened to the filthy conversation of the Sodomites. Many years later, the apostle Peter described how God ". . . delivered just Lot, vexed with the filthy conversation of the wicked. (For that righteous man dwelling among them, in seeing and hearing vexed his righteous soul from day to day with their unlawful deeds)" (2 Peter 2:7–8). It is difficult to understand how any righteous man could grieve without making an attempt to escape from the circumstances which threatened his existence. Lot consented to the wedding of his two daughters even though he knew the bridegrooms were homosexuals. When he offered to deliver his daughters to a lustful mob, it was said the young women were virgins (see Gen. 19:8). Those filthy men only desired slaves who could cook and clean houses. They satisfied their lustful desires by cohabiting with men. All those sickening events grieved Lot, but he made no effort to leave the city and renew the fellowship which earlier had enriched his soul.

During the ministry of the Savior, a wealthy young ruler came to enquire about receiving eternal life but, when he knew the cost of discipleship, went away sorrowful. Lot's condemnation was greater; he could have taken his herds as he left the city of Sodom. Probably, he would have increased his wealth had he moved along the shores of the Sea of Galilee where serenity was at least possible. It was said that "By faith, Moses, when he was come to years, refused to be called the son of Pharaoh's daughter; Choosing rather to suffer affliction with the people of God, than to enjoy the pleasures of sin for a season; Esteeming the reproach of Christ greater riches than the treasures in Egypt" (Heb. 11:24–26). The glorious example provided by the patriarch was a striking contrast to the actions of the disappointing nephew of Abram. It is doubtful whether Lot ever pleased God, but any spiritual influence he possessed was lost in Sodom. Even Simon Peter discovered it was dangerous to remain at the enemy's fire.

The Man Who Lost His Fortune . . . *Devastating*

"And when the morning arose, then the angels hastened Lot, saying, Arise, take thy wife, and thy two daughters, which are here; lest thou be consumed in the iniquity of the city. And while he lingered, the men laid hold upon his hand, and upon the hand of his wife, and upon the hand of his two daughters; the LORD being merciful unto him: and they brought him forth and set him without the city. And it came to pass, when they had brought them forth abroad, that he (the angel) said, Escape for thy life; look not behind thee, neither stay thou in all the plain; escape to the mountain, lest thou be consumed. And Lot said unto them, Oh, not so, my Lord" (Gen. 19:15–18).

Many years ago I was entertained in the home of an Australian, Walter Beasly, who at that time financially supported much of the archaeological work being done around the world. We were speaking about liberal theologians who deny the accuracy of certain Bible stories. My friend said, "Yes. They criticized the account of the destruction of Sodom and Gomorrah, but we know now how it happened. Beneath the ground upon which those cities stood, a burned-out oil field had been discovered, and on either end vertical faults were found in the strata of the earth. Throughout the area enormous amounts of rock salt exist deep in the earth, but around the sites of the ancient cities the salt is on the surface. The Dead Sea is a notable example of that fact. The countryside was shaken by an earthquake; Sodom and Gomorrah slipped between the faults placing enormous pressure upon the oil field. The tremendous upsurge pushed the salt into the atmosphere where it disintegrated and fell as a gigantic snowstorm. The cities were destroyed by the oil-fed fires, but when Lot's wife turned to see her home, the earth began to split, and she was unable to proceed or retreat. The poor woman was overwhelmed and died of suffocation—she became a pillar of salt. . . ." My Australian friend concluded his remarks by saying, "Scholars no longer deny the accuracy of that ancient story; they know how it happened."

Within moments Lot's cattle disappeared, and their owner was left with nothing but haunting memories. When his father died, the son had little if any wealth, but after the destruction of Sodom, he had nothing! What might have happened had he remained with Abram, close to God?

The Man Who Lost His Future . . . *Disastrous*

"And Lot went up out of Zoar, and dwelt in the mountain, and his two daughters with him; for he feared to dwell in Zoar: and dwelt in a cave, he and his two daughters" (Gen. 19:30). He had left God's hills a very wealthy man; he returned a pauper. His dwelling place became a cavern of memories. The final details concerning this desperate man related to nocturnal visits made by his anxious daughters. The man who might have been a friend of God became so drunk he was unable to recognize the women who shared his bed (see Gen. 19:31–36). Lot stained the pages of history with debauchery and lust. Things would have been different had he spoken with God instead of the men of Sodom.

Yet one brilliant star shone during his nights of failure; his uncle Abram continued to love him, and when enemies carried Lot into slavery, Abram rescued him and restored all that had been confiscated. When the cities of the plain were about to be destroyed, it was the same faithful friend who interceded for his safety. "And it came to pass, when God destroyed the cities of the plain, that God remembered Abraham, and sent Lot out of the midst of the overthrow, when he overthrew the cities in which Lot dwelt (Gen. 19:29).

It has often been claimed that nothing is new! Even in the Garden of Eden, Jehovah demonstrated there were two directions in which people could travel. They could obey God or please themselves. The story of Abraham and his nephew revealed that men can remain in the everlasting hills or waste their lives among evil associates in the plains of illicit pleasure. Solomon said, "There is a way which seemeth right unto a man, but the end thereof are the ways of death" (Prov. 14:12). The Lord said, "Enter ye in at the strait gate: for wide is the gate, and broad is the way, that leadeth to destruction, and many there be which go in thereat: Because strait is the gate, and narrow is the way, which leadeth unto life, and few there be that find it" (Matt. 7:13–14). Joshua, believing these facts necessitated choice, said to his people, "Choose you this day whom ye will serve . . ." (Josh. 24:15). The air is always cleaner on a mountain top than in a valley filled with smog! Mrs. Rhea F. Miller was inspired when she wrote:

> I'd rather have Jesus than silver or gold,
> I'd rather be His, than have riches untold;
> I'd rather have Jesus than houses or land:
> I'd rather be led by His nail pierced hand.
> Than to be the king of a vast domain,
> Or be held in sin's dread sway.
> I'd rather have Jesus than anything
> This world affords today.

Long ago, one of Job's friends said, "Canst thou by searching find out God? canst thou find out the Almighty unto perfection? It is as high as heaven; what canst thou do? deeper than hell; what canst thou know? The measure thereof is longer than the earth, and broader than the sea" (Job 11:7–9). The ancient philosopher's conception of Jehovah suggested that Job could never clearly understand the God he professed to serve. Many people would disagree with that opinion, for they have learned to see God in a flower, hear His music in the songs of the birds, recognize His artistry in sunrises and sunsets, and feel the warmth of His love in the Person of His Son, the Lord Jesus Christ. Jehovah is no longer an inscrutable Deity existing and reigning in distant heavens; He is close to all who call upon Him. Nevertheless, there is reason to believe He is best seen in little things—in the circumstances by which people are surrounded daily.

A Revelation of Divine Tenderness

"*And I will send hornets before thee, which shall drive out the Hivite, the Canaanite, and the Hittite, from before thee*" (Ex. 23:28). The children of Israel were on their way to Canaan. The bondage endured in Egypt had become an unpleasant memory. The future seemed to be bright with prospect and hope, yet the undisciplined Hebrews had no experience in warfare, and their enemies were likely to benefit from that fact. Moses had been specially trained, but unfortunately he could not do everything. The Lord was aware of this, but He had many assistants. The wilderness was the home of myriads of winged nuisances, and even they responded to the suggestions of the Almighty. The children of Israel should have understood that fact, for they had seen how the plagues of frogs and lice paralyzed the Egyptians. If swarms of hornets went ahead of the advancing Hebrews, their rapier-like stings could easily strike terror into the hearts of all they attacked. There is no conclusive evidence that the "hornets" were insects. The absence of references in the historical books of the Old Testament lends credence to the interpretation that they were kings at war among themselves, that God overruled in the affairs of men to protect His beloved people. It is interesting to note that God speaking through Joshua said to His people, "And I sent the hornet before you, which drave them out from before you, even the two kings of the Amorites; but not with thy sword, nor with thy bow" (Josh. 24:12). Most theologians believe the hornets could have been difficulties of many kinds, that adverse circumstances terrified the enemies, and thus the safety of Israel was assured.

It is wise to remember that God's care for His people is unending. "Like as a father pitieth his children, so the LORD pitieth them that fear him" (Ps. 103:13). The fact that Jehovah commanded His people to advance even when the sea blocked their pathway to freedom was evidence that He would divide the sea and make obedience to His command possible (see Ex. 14:15). When Adam and Eve were expelled from the garden of Eden, God went with them. When Israel left Egypt, they did not go alone. The Almighty accompanied them, and although the people disappointed Him, He never abandoned them. As they journeyed through the wilderness, Jehovah knew they were incapable of overcoming their enemies, so special "hornets" became their advance guards. It was written, "But the mercy of the LORD is from everlasting to everlasting upon them that fear him, and his righteousness unto children's children" (Ps. 103:17). God never changes, and it is stimulating to remember that the text includes all generations. Men are never expected to do anything alone, for even in the most critical emergencies the Lord abides with His people. "The eternal God is thy refuge, and underneath are the everlasting arms" (Deut. 33:27).

A Revelation of God's Thoughtfulness

". . . I will not drive them out from before thee in one year; lest the land become desolate, and the beast of the field multiply against thee" (Ex. 23:29). Had Jehovah so desired, He could have instantly exterminated all the enemies, but sometimes delayed blessings are the greatest of all benedictions. If children were not placed upon their feet, they would never learn to walk. The conquest of Canaan would not be easy, but to cultivate the land, keep at bay the wild animals, and at the same time to survive in strange surroundings would require endless fortitude and patience. Men do not mature overnight. Every enemy stronghold was surrounded by fertile land, the product of unceasing labor. If the Canaanites had been annihilated, the land would have become a wilderness before the Hebrews could possess it. Many years were to pass before God's people would occupy their inheritance, and until that day arrived, the local inhabitants would act as caretakers. Lions and other dangerous beasts would be controlled, and in an indirect way the future of the nation would be assured. Evidently, God foresaw every need of His people and with continuing wisdom planned their protection. God is wiser than people; humans think only of the moment. The Lord Who sees the end from the beginning knows how to plan for the future and is never surprised. Judas thought only of the transient and lost his soul; Annanias and Sapphira thought only of wealth and never lived to spend their money. Yet, "Moses, when he was come to years refused to be called the son of Pharaoh's daughter; Choosing rather to suffer affliction with the people of God, than to enjoy the pleasures of sin for a season; Esteeming the reproach of Christ greater riches than the treasures in Egypt" (Heb. 11:24–26).

Sometimes it is difficult to understand the delays of the Lord, and many people would like Him to act more quickly. Nevertheless, God knows what He is doing and is extremely capable of handling the affairs of all who trust Him.

A Revelation of God's Thoroughness

"*By little and little I will drive them out from before thee, until thou be increased, and will inherit the land*" (Ex. 23:30). Sometimes the outflow of divine energy is regulated by the appreciation of the people to whom it is sent. Need begets prayer; affluence and excessive success beget independence and forgetfulness. The Lord disciplines His children even as human fathers do their offspring. Some people are better Christians in trouble than when their circumstances are serene and pleasing. The disciples of Jesus learned more in the storm-tossed boat than they would have on the shore. Children never become adults overnight, and students do not graduate after one lesson! "Little by little" seems to be God's way of delivering, helping, and controlling His people. The poet was inspired when he wrote, "O God our help in ages past; Our hope for years to come." Another writer said, "I need Thee every hour, most gracious Lord." But the man closest to reality said, "Moment by moment, I've light from above." To walk with the Lord is better than to visit Him at some unique festival. The refiner gives special attention to his work when dross is being removed from the molten metal. When the gold reflects his image, he knows his task has been completed. God is very thorough! Blessed are the people who never complain!

A Revelation of God's Truthfulness

Many years had passed since the original promises were made to God's people. Unfortunately, disobedience and lack of faith had prevented Israel from occupying the land, and the tribes had wandered from place to place in the wilderness. Someone said, "It took one night to get Israel out of Egypt, but forty years to get Egypt out of Israel." Yet finally, Joshua led a new generation into the Promised Land. When he reminisced, God said to him, *"And ye went over Jordan and came unto Jericho, and the men of Jericho fought against you, the Amorites, and the Perizzites, and the Canaanites, and the Hittites, and the Girgashites, the Hivites, and the Jebusites; and I delivered them into your hand. And I sent the hornet before you, which drave them out from before you, even the two kings of the Amorites, but not with thy sword or with thy bow. And I have given you a land for which ye did not labor, and cities which ye built not, and ye dwell in them; of the vineyards and oliveyards which ye planted not do ye eat. Now therefore fear the Lord, and serve him in sincerity and in truth"* (Josh. 24:11–14). What God had promised decades earlier He faithfully fulfilled. The hornets—whatever they were—had completed their mission and the Promised Land had been possessed. That wonderful fact begat responsibility, and therefore, Joshua urged his followers to abandon their idols. Jehovah, who had accomplished so much on their behalf, deserved to be honored. He had not failed; neither should they.

Christians should look back with gratitude, up with praise, and onward with courage. The children of Israel could never repay the debt of love they owed, and neither can we. There is always cause to return thanks.

> O Thou whose bounty fills my cup,
> With every blessing meet!
> I give Thee thanks for every drop—
> The bitter and the sweet.
> I praise Thee for the desert road,
> And for the river side,
> For all, Thy goodness hath bestowed,
> And all, Thy grace denied.
> I thank Thee for both smile and frown,
> And for the gain and loss:
> I praise Thee for the future crown,

And for the present cross.
I thank Thee for both wings of love
Which stirred my worldly nest
And for the stormy clouds which drove
Me trembling to Thy breast.
I bless Thee for the glad increase,
And for the waning joy:
And for this strange, this settled peace
Which nothing can destroy.

Author Unknown

"And there were certain men who were defiled by the dead body of a man, that they could not keep the passover on that day: and they came before Moses and before Aaron on that day: And those men said unto him, We are defiled by the dead body of a man: wherefore are we kept back, that we may not offer an offering of the LORD in his appointed season among the children of Israel? And Moses said unto them, Stand still, and I will hear what the LORD will command concerning you" (Num. 9:6–8).

It is refreshing to discover that Solomon did not know everything, and even Moses realized there were things he needed to learn (see Prov. 30:18–19). The man who has no need of improvement has outlived his usefulness. The Passover, the most important feast in Israel, was solemnly observed on the fourteenth day of the first month. "And the LORD spake unto Moses in the wilderness of Sinai, in the first month of the second year after they were come out of the land of Egypt, saying, Let the children of Israel also keep the passover at his appointed season. In the fourteenth day of this month, at even, ye shall keep it in his appointed season; according to all the rites of it, and according to all the ceremonies thereof, shall ye keep it. And Moses spake unto the children of Israel, that they should keep the passover. And they kept the passover on the fourteenth day of the first month at even in the wilderness of Sinai: according to all that the Lord commanded Moses, so did the children of Israel" (Num. 9:1–5).

The Problem and the Prayer . . . *Guilt Excluding*

Attendance at the Passover was mandatory for all men. Every male was commanded to obey the commandment of God, and failure to do so was regarded as sinful. This was considered by the Hebrews to be a delight and a solemn duty. When these details were explained to the nation, certain men came to Moses to ask a very important question. People who were defiled were strictly forbidden to participate in the feast, and travelers who were unable to reach home in time for the celebrations were deprived of their greatest privilege. This appeared to be unjust, and the men who complained to Moses asked if an alternative could be found.

Their leader had no idea what to say. He had never been confronted by that problem and hesitated before giving an answer.

"And Moses said unto them, Stand still, and I will hear what the LORD will command concerning you" (Num. 9:8). That situation was challenging. Four facts await investigation.

(1) *Their Defilement—"We are defiled by the dead body of a man."* This contact might not have been intentional. Additional details were never supplied by the ancient writer, but the uncleanliness might have been caused accidentally or by some unknown humanitarian reason. The men asking the question might have been visiting a sick friend who died during their stay. Such a situation would have prohibited attendance at the feast. The same fact applies to all people who are unworthy to share fellowship with God. It is written, "For all have sinned and come short of the glory of God" (Rom. 3:23). The prophet Isaiah said, "All we like sheep have gone astray; we have turned every one to his own way" (Isa. 53:6). Wise men do not argue with God; they believe His Word and pray as did the publican, ". . . God be merciful to me a sinner" (Luke 18:13).

(2) *Their Directions—"Wherefore are we kept back . . ."* The Pharisee mentioned by Christ tried to justify himself before God by enumerating his virtuous deeds. Jesus said, "The Pharisee stood and prayed thus with himself, God, I thank thee, that I am not as other men are, extortioners, unjust, adulterers, or even as this publican. I fast twice in the week, I give tithes of all that I possess" (Luke 18:11–12). The men who questioned Moses did not deny their predicament; they recognized the authority of the Almighty and endeavored to discover what might be done to solve their problem. They were wise, and so are all people who learn from their example. If there were a way by which favor could be found, they wished to know about it, and for that purpose they came to Moses who could enquire on their behalf. They desired to worship at the feast and were willing to do anything to promote that possibility.

(3) *Their Desire—". . . an offering of the LORD in his appointed place."* The questioners were sincere and anxious to know what God required. With intensity of purpose they desired to find means by which to share God's benediction and join other people in remembering the amazing deliverance from Egypt. They were anxious to give. Travelers prevented from returning in time for the festivities wished to know if their absence could be overlooked or remedied and wanted to know if Moses could solve their problem. They seemed to say, "We can purchase our lamb and are willing to observe all the commandments, but, Moses, how can we do this?"

Their leader became their intercessor, and God answered his prayer. David said, "Blessed are they that keep his testimonies, and that seek him *with the whole heart*" (Ps. 119:2).

(4)   *Their Decision—"And those men said unto him . . ."* Procrastination is considered to be the thief of time, but the ancient Hebrews were desperate and did not postpone action until a later date. They came to the servant of God and their effort was rewarded. It is never wise to put off until tomorrow something that needs attention today. The patriarch had never previously considered this problem. Many years later, Jesus was confronted by a similar situation.

"And it came to pass, that, as they went in the way, a certain man said unto him, Lord, I will follow thee whithersoever thou goest. And Jesus said unto him, Foxes have holes, and birds of the air have nests; but the Son of man hath not where to lay his head. And he said unto another, Follow me. But he said, Lord suffer me first to go and bury my father. Jesus said unto him, Let the dead bury their dead: but go thou and preach the kingdom of God. And another also said, Lord, I will follow thee; but let me first go bid them farewell, which are at home at my house. And Jesus said unto him, No man, having put his hand to the plough, and looking back, is fit for the kingdom of God" (Luke 9:57–62). People with doubts and problems should accept God's invitation, "Come *now*, and let us reason together, saith the LORD: though your sins be as scarlet, they shall be as white as snow; though they be red like crimson, they shall be as wool" (Isa. 1:18).

The Provision and the Privilege . . . *God Explaining*

"And the LORD spake unto Moses, saying, Speak unto the children of Israel, saying, If any man of you or of your posterity shall be unclean by reason of a dead body, or be in a journey afar off, yet he shall keep the passover unto the LORD. The fourteenth day of the second month at even they shall keep it, and eat it with unleavened bread and bitter herbs. . . . But the man that is clean, and is not in a journey, and forbeareth to keep the passover, even the same soul shall be cut off from among his people: because he brought not the offering of the LORD in his appointed season, that man shall bear his sin" (Num. 9:9–13).

The arrangement for a second passover was one of the most gracious acts of the Almighty; it provided a thirty-day period of grace in which men could prepare to enjoy the ordinance of which they had been deprived. It unified law and love and foreshadowed the link between Mount Sinai and Calvary.

(1) *God's Desire.* When Jehovah responded to the request of Moses, it became evident that He also wished to share the passover with His believing people. Uncleanness was not an excuse for avoiding the feast; there was always a way by which suppliants could be cleansed from defilement. Likewise, a man who was clean could not be pardoned for inexcusable neglect. The statement "that man shall bear his sin" was ominous. It was better to be unclean and know it than to be clean and indifferent. Since the beginning of time it has always been possible for sinful people to approach God and obtain forgiveness. Unfortunately, some people ignore God's commandments and do as they please.

(2) *God's Delight.* Samuel said, "Hath the LORD as great delight in burnt offerings and sacrifices, as in obeying the voice of the LORD? Behold, to obey is better than sacrifice, and to hearken than the fat of rams" (1 Sam. 15:22). Each commandment encouraged virtue and supplied a way of expressing love to God. The Israelites did not willingly make bricks in Egypt; they had no choice—they were slaves. The boy who offered his lunch to Jesus gave voluntarily and joyfully. It would be difficult to decide who was the happier, the lad who gave or the Lord who received. As a father delights in the obedience of his children, so God is pleased when men and women seek His fellowship.

(3) *God's Disapproval.* Jehovah always went the "extra mile" when offering mercy to undeserving sinners. The thirty days of grace indicated that He was anxious to assist believers in celebrating the passover. The same mercy was extended after Noah entered the ark. The vessel was ready to sail; the door had been closed and the final tasks completed. "And it came to pass *after seven days*, that the waters of the flood were upon the earth" (Gen. 7:10). Similarly, the Lord provided a month in which men could prepare to attend the second passover. If they did not avail themselves of this wonderful opportunity, their condemnation was justified. The New Testament writer expressed a similar thought when he said, "How shall we escape, if we neglect so great salvation; which at the first began to be spoken by the Lord, and was confirmed unto us by them that heard him?" (Heb. 2:3). Wise men obeyed the command of Moses, "But the man that is clean, and is not in a journey, and

30

forbeareth to keep the passover, even the same soul shall be cut off from among his people because he brought not the offering of the Lord in his appointed season—*that man shall bear his sin*" (Num. 9:13).

The Partnership and the Pleasure . . . *Guests Expected*

"And if a stranger shall sojourn among you, and will keep the passover unto the LORD; according to the ordinance of the passover, and according to the manner thereof, so shall he do: ye shall have one ordinance, both for the stranger, and for him that was born in the land" (Num. 9:14).

The new instructions given to Moses were surprising, for once again God extended His mercy. Normally, Jews were the only people permitted to observe the passover. "And the LORD said to Moses and Aaron, This is the ordinance of the passover: There shall no stranger eat thereof. But every man's servant that is bought for money, when thou hast circumcised him, then he shall eat thereof. *A foreigner and an hired servant shall not eat thereof*" (Ex. 12:43–45). Probably at the time when God spoke to Moses, the children of Israel had no contact with people of other nations. As years passed, the influence of the Jews spread; "strangers" were attracted by God's chosen people, and at least some identified themselves with the chosen race. Many years later God saw the need of revising the former commandments and issued an edict which permitted strangers to keep the feast in fellowship with their Hebrew hosts. Circumcision was the only unchanging condition; it was the evidence that Israel was a separated nation. It was a thrilling moment when "*those born in the land*" sat together with "*the strangers from afar,*" and masters and slaves became brethren. The wealth of the owner did not enhance his chance of finding favor with God, and slaves were not deprived of the divine benediction.

Many years later Paul expressed the same truth when he wrote to the Ephesian Christians. "Now therefore ye are no more strangers and foreigners, but fellowcitizens with the saints, and of the household of God; And are built upon the foundation of the apostles and prophets, Jesus Christ himself being the chief corner stone; In whom all the building fitly framed together groweth unto an holy temple in the Lord: In whom ye also are builded together for an habitation of God through the Spirit" (Eph. 2:19–22).

It is reasonable to believe that when God issued His commandments to Moses, He was, so to speak, painting on human canvas a scene which He saw developing in the distant future. The slain lamb was a forerunner of the Lamb of God, and the passover feast was emblematic of the communion service in which believers gratefully remembered their redemption purchased by the blood of the Savior. Throughout the Old Testament dispensations the slain lamb was the center of all religious practice. During the present age everything of value revolves around the risen Christ; without His presence religion deteriorates into cold formality. No Jewish sacrifice was ever resurrected, "But now is Christ risen from the dead, and become the firstfruits of them that slept" (1 Cor. 15:20).

HOBAB, THE MAN WHO REFUSED TO GO TO CANAAN

"And Moses said unto Hobab, the son of Raguel the Midianite, Moses' father in law, We are journeying unto the place of which the Lord said, I will give it you: come thou with us, and we will do thee good; for the Lord hath spoken good concerning Israel. And he said unto him, I will not go; but I will depart to mine own land, and to my kindred" (Num. 10:29–30).

There has always been a mystery associated with Hobab who visited Moses as the children of Israel journeyed from Egypt to Canaan. Hebrew scholars believe he was the son of Jethro, the former priest of Midian, who gave his daughter in marriage to the fugitive Moses. The ancient record says, "But Moses fled from the face of Pharaoh, and dwelt in the land of Midian: and he sat down by a well. Now the priest of Midian had seven daughters; and they came and drew water, and filled the troughs to water their father's flock. And the shepherds came and drove them away: but Moses stood up and helped them, and watered their flock. And when they came to Reuel their father, he said, How is that ye are come so soon today? And they said, An Egyptian delivered us out of the hand of the shepherds, and also drew water enough for us, and watered the flock. And he said unto his daughters, And where is he? why is it that ye have left the man? call him, that he may eat bread. And Moses was content to dwell with the man: and he gave Moses Zipporah his daughter. And she bare him a son, and he called his name Gershom: for he said: I have been a stranger in a strange land" (Ex. 2:15–22).

It appears that Hobab had inherited his father's title, and when Moses returned to Egypt, he was probably among those who bade him farewell as he commenced his journey. Years later, he welcomed the opportunity to visit his sister and her husband, and the reunion caused much rejoicing. It may be assumed that the two men reminisced about earlier times and remembered the days when the daughters were delivered from the annoying shepherds. It was never revealed how long the visitor remained with his brother-in-law, but evidently the patriarch was delighted to entertain his wife's brother, and Moses and Zipporah wondered how they could convince their visitor to accompany them on the journey to the Land of Promise. The nation did not require a guide, for Jehovah had made arrangements to supply that need. The ancient author said, "And the cloud of the LORD was upon them by day, when they went out of the camp" (Num. 10:34). Israel's leader knew that without some valid reason, Hobab would never consent to abandon his home and people. He therefore gave much thought to the problem and, recognizing the wilderness was the natural habitat of the Midianites, used that fact to influence the man whose presence was desired. When Hobab refused to accept the initial invitation, Moses said, "Leave us not, I pray thee, forasmuch as thou knowest how we are to encamp in the wilderness, *and thou mayest be to us instead of eyes*" (Num. 10:31). It is not known whether Hobab consented to journey to Canaan. Perhaps he did, and maybe he did not. This wonderful story from antiquity expressed the New Testament in an Old Testament era.

The Grand Pilgrimage . . . *"We are journeying"*

Moses was convinced about certain things; he knew where the nation had been and where it was going. Somewhere beyond the horizon God had prepared a country in which His people could be free. His followers were determined to reach that destination. The statement "we are journeying" expressed all that needed to be said.

Throughout the history of the church, Christians have used that ancient illustration. The writer to the Hebrews said, "For here have we no continuing city, but we seek one to come" (Heb. 13:14). Paul endorsed the statement when he wrote, "For our conversation (citizenship) is in heaven" (Phil. 3:20). The Living Bible and other translations interpret the text, "But our homeland is in heaven." The apostle taught that through the merits of Christ, God redeemed sinners to Himself and brought them from slavery to freedom. The desire of the church has always been that ultimately the journey to heaven will be completed through divine grace. Samuel Stenneet expressed that truth when he wrote:

> On Jordan's stormy banks I stand,
> And cast a wistful eye
> To Canaan's fair and happy land,
> Where my possessions lie.
>
> I am bound for the promised land:
> I am bound for the promised land.
> Oh, who will come and go with me?
> I am bound for the promised land.

The Gracious Plea . . . *"Come thou with us"*

"Come, with us, and we will do thee good; for the LORD hath spoken good concerning Israel" (Num. 10:29). The friendship between Moses and the family of Zipporah his wife was very evident. Jethro the priest of Midian had welcomed the fugitive from Egypt, had given consent for the marriage of his daughter, and had become the proud grandfather of two boys, Gershom and Eliezer. As often as possible, the priest visited his family, and their fellowship was delightful. If Hobab were the son of that man, he was well known among the Hebrews and greatly loved by his sister. There were valid reasons why Moses desired his company on the journey to the promised land.

(1) *The Offer of Salvation.* Every Israelite knew that Jehovah was doing something unusual for His people. He had delivered the slaves from Egypt and intended to complete what had been commenced. The entire nation would eventually enter the land of milk and honey. There would be difficulties along the way; many battles would be fought and won, but nothing could prevent the ultimate triumph. When Moses issued the invitation to his wife's brother, he did something not usually permitted. The Midianites were aliens and therefore had no claim upon the Almighty. If New Testament language can be permitted, Hobab was a sinner to whom was extended the offer of salvation. As his sister had become one of the chosen people, so he was given the chance to belong to the family of God.

(2) *The Opportunity to Serve.* Hobab had been reared in the wilderness; he knew the terrain, the water holes, and how to survive in the desert. Moses knew God was able to sustain His people. The cloud above the tabernacle would lead them safely to their destination. Yet he also knew that the services of his brother-in-law could be of great value. He could be as eyes to the nation, and his wisdom could assist in solving the smaller problems which arose daily. The patriarch remembered the time when he had been the only judge in Israel. His father-in-law had suggested that other judges be appointed to handle the less important problems, and that wise procedure prevented many headaches for the overworked leader of the people. Moses remembered these things and believed the son would emulate the example given by his father.

(3) *The Obtaining of Satisfaction.* Moses and his wife loved Hobab; their personal happiness would be increased by his fellow-

ship. If he could be persuaded to remain with the people of God, the family would be delighted. Together they could serve Jehovah and receive His benediction. Probably, Moses and Zipporah discussed how best they could persuade their visitor to remain, and when the invitation was given, their prayers went with it. A positive reply would necessitate many changes, but God was offering much more than could be estimated. David said, "I had rather be a doorkeeper in the house of my God, than to dwell in the tents of wickedness" (Ps. 84:10). Moses believed it would be infinitely better to be a suppliant in Israel than to be a priest in Midian.

The Glorious Promise . . . *"We will do thee good"*

During the early part of His ministry the Savior said, "But seek ye first the kingdom of God, and his righteousness; and all these things shall be added unto you" (Matt. 6:33). His statement expressed a truth which had been evident from the commencement of time. No man ever worked for God without being rewarded generously. The Lord always returned more than He received.

(1) *The Reward of Sacrifice . . . Salvation.* If Hobab had accepted the invitation to become the co-worker of Moses, his life would have been revolutionized. His work as the priest of Midian would have terminated immediately. The subsequent history and death of the Midianites was terrible. The thirty-first chapter of the book of Numbers describes how they were slaughtered; their sins were so horrendous in God's sight, that He could not tolerate their existence. The ultimate fate of Hobab is unknown, but if he remained among his people, he perished. The offer made by Moses indicated that acceptance would have led to a salvation, the importance of which could never be estimated. It has always been God's will to rescue perishing souls, but when His offer of mercy is declined, sinners are doomed!

(2) *The Reward of Surrender . . . Safety.* "And Moab said unto the elders of Midian, Now shall this company lick up all that are round about us, as the ox licketh up the grass of the field. And Balak the son of Zippor was king of the Moabites at that time. He sent messengers therefore unto Balaam the son of Beor to Pethor, which is by the river of the land of the children of his people, to call him, saying, Behold there is a people come out from Egypt: behold they cover the face of the earth, and they abide over against me: Come now therefore, I pray thee, curse me this people; for they are

too mighty for me" (Num. 22:4–7). From that time forward things deteriorated so quickly that finally God permitted disease to harass the people and many died. After the slaughter of the Midianites only virgins survived.

God saw the end from the beginning, and when Hobab was invited to become associated with His people, the Lord was providing an escape unprecedented in those times. Once again it must be affirmed this was an indication of what existed in His mind. He always provides an escape from destruction, but man's cooperation is a vital necessity if salvation is to become a reality within the souls of men and women. When we accept God's offer, the Lord assumes responsibility for our safety. The Savior said, "My sheep hear my voice, and I know them, and they follow me: And I give unto them eternal life; and *they shall never perish, neither shall any man pluck them out of my hand*" (John 10:27–28).

(3) *The Reward of Service . . . Satisfaction.* Moses said to his brother-in-law, "Come thou with us, and we will do thee good." Later he repeated his promise, saying, "And it shall be, if thou go with us . . . that what goodness the Lord shall do unto us, the same will we do unto thee" (Num. 10:32). The integrity of God and the honor of Moses were united to that promise. Hobab's services would be rewarded; he would share equally with the Hebrews the benediction which fell upon the nation.

Paul informed the Christians in Corinth that their works would be tried in the fires of God's scrutiny, and whatever had been done for the Savior would be honored. Their eternal compensation would exceed any loss sustained on earth (see 1 Cor. 3:13–15). The Lord also said, "Whosoever shall give to drink unto one of these little ones a cup of cold water only in the name of a disciple, verily I say unto you, he shall in no wise lose his reward" (Matt. 10:42). If Hobab had agreed to serve among the people of God, he would have reaped rewards beyond imagination. The writer to the Hebrews said, "For God is not unrighteous to forget your work and labor of love, which ye have shewed toward his name, in that ye have ministered to the saints, and do minister" (Heb. 6:10).

The Great Problem . . . "*I will not go, but will depart to mine own land*"

Hobab's refusal to accompany Moses and the children of Israel on their journey to Canaan was a disappointment to everyone concerned. The reply was apparently swift, concise, and definite. He had plans for the future, and neither the persistence of Moses nor love for Zipporah would change that decision; his word was final! It would be informative to discover the reasons for his refusal.

(1) *His Fame . . . Was he unwilling to lose his importance?* His father Jethro had been the priest of Midian, and since most titles and offices were hereditary, Hobab had probably become the religious leader of his people. If that deduction is correct, then he was an important man among the Midianites, who would seek his counsel and follow his advice. He was possibly a very rich man, for his engagements would be lucrative; his clients would reward his services. He was second only to the king, and it would have been difficult to leave his home to become a pilgrim in a very inhospitable wilderness. The children of Israel did not need a priest. Aaron and his sons did their work in the Tabernacle, and a priest of Midian would not be accepted in Israel.

Many years later, a rich young ruler asked the Savior about the possibility of obtaining eternal life, but the Lord's reply shattered his interest. Jesus said, "Sell all that thou hast, and distribute unto the poor, and thou shalt have treasure in heaven; and come, follow me" (Luke 18:22). There was very little difference between the man who came to Moses and the ruler who talked with Jesus.

(2) *His Family . . . Was he unwilling to leave his friends?* Hobab said, "I will depart to mine own land, and to my kindred." He refused to emulate his sister's example. When Zipporah was given in marriage to the man from Egypt, she left her father and mother and accompanied her husband to an unknown destination. A similar attitude was evident when a man said to the Savior, "Lord, suffer me first to go and bury my father" (Luke 9:59). Someone said, "Unless Christ be Lord of all, He is not Lord at all!" Lot refused to leave Sodom and as a consequence nearly lost his life. Jesus said, "For where your treasure is, there will your heart be also" (see Matt. 6:21). Hobab's heart was evidently with his friends and family in Midian; he preferred their company to that of Moses and his followers. Unfortunately, many people have made a similar choice.

(3) *His Future . . . Was he unwilling to risk his life?* As a leader of the nation, Hobab would have had a beautiful and desirable home. His wealth guaranteed comfort of every kind, but had he

38

accepted the invitation given by Moses, everything would have changed dramatically. A warm bed in his own home was preferable to a tent in a wilderness. His permanent home, whether it was a Bedouin's tent or a more substantial residence, was far better than marching continually toward a distant land. It was unreasonable to ask a man to leave everything for nothing! The traveling Hebrews would have to fight for the land they hoped to possess; many lives would be lost as the struggle continued. Why should Hobab be engulfed in wars in which he had no interest? "Let the Hebrews fight their own battles; I want to live in peace among my friends." It is difficult to read and consider the words of that man without remembering the message of Christ. He said, "If any man will come after me, let him deny himself, and take up his cross, and follow me. For whosoever shall save his life shall lose it; and whosoever will lose his life for my sake shall find it" (Matt. 16:24–25). It may cost a lot to become a disciple of Christ; but it costs even more to refuse.

The Gentle Persuasion . . . "And Moses said: Leave us not, I pray thee."

The final episode of this enthralling story was never recorded for posterity, but Moses did not give up easily. He refused to accept a negative answer and tried to change the mind of his stubborn brother-in-law. Some theologians believe he succeeded; others think he did not. The Bible says, "And they departed from the mount of the Lord." Was Hobab included in that statement, or was the historian merely adding to his manuscript? Perhaps the second attempt to convince the Midianite succeeded; maybe he did accompany Moses to the Promised Land, but on the other hand, he could have returned to his home in Midian. Whatever happened remains a mystery, but Hobab made his own decision. Men may be invited to become pilgrims, but God never forces His will upon reluctant people. It may be significant that the writer to the Hebrews on three occasions said, "Today, if ye will hear his voice, Harden not your hearts" (Heb. 3:7–8, 15; 4:7).

THE EAGLE—GOD'S SERMON IN THE SKY

"As an eagle stirreth up her nest, fluttereth over her young, spreadeth abroad her wings, taketh them, beareth them on her wings: So the LORD *alone did lead him, and there was no strange god with him"*
(Deut. 32:11–12).

The eagle is the most majestic of all birds mentioned in the Scriptures, and according to the Zondervan Encyclopedia of the Bible, there are still twelve different kinds found in Israel. There is also the Egyptian vulture, which is one of the most repulsive creatures in existence. G. S. Cansdale says, "Palestine is rich in these birds [the eagles]. There are golden; spotted; lesser spotted; Bonelli's booted; imperial; tawny; Verraux's; short toed; white tailed; black bearded and Griffon. . . . Three species breed in tall trees, or more often, on cliffs. The others are passing migrants or winter visitors. They feed mostly on live prey, which ranges from young deer to reptiles and insects." There are numerous references in the Bible to these wonderful birds that were known for their strength, speed, beauty, and care for their young. It was generally believed among the ancient Hebrews that the parent birds deliberately broke up their nests and, carrying their young, dropped them, only to catch them again on their broad wings. This method taught the eaglets how to fly. Some scholars have said there is no evidence this idea was based on fact.

Dr. W. M. Thompson, who was one of the greatest authorities on Palestine, wrote, "The notion however, appears to have been prevalent among the ancients that the eagle did actually take up her timid young, and carry them forth to embolden them, and teach them how to use their own pinions. To this idea, Moses seems to refer in Exodus 19:4: 'Ye have seen what I did unto the Egyptians, and how I bare you on eagles' wings, and brought you unto myself.' *The fact is not impossible*; the eagle is strong enough to do it, but I am not aware that such a thing has ever been witnessed. I myself, however, have seen the old eagle fly *round and round the nest, and back and forth past it, while the young ones fluttered and shivered on the edge, as if eager, but afraid to launch forth from the giddy precipice.* And no wonder, for the nest is 'on high', and a fall from thence would end their flight forever.

"If Moses were not the author of Job, they seem both to have been familiar with this bird and its habits. One illusion is very striking: *'Her eyes behold afar off'* (Job 39:29). The power of vision in the eagle is amazing; almost incredible. No sooner does a kid fall in the wilderness among the thick bushes, than some of these keen-sighted hunters after prey notice it from their pathway in mid-heaven, and, circling round and round, pounce down upon, and bear it away to their nest. This appears to be done purely by sight" (quoted from *The Land and the Book*, W. M. Thompson, p. 151, published by Thomas Nelson and Sons, London, England, 1910). Certain Bible verses imply that what Dr. Thompson admitted could be true was accepted as fact by Hebrew writers.

God's Undeserved Compassion . . . *Amazing* (Exodus 19:4)

"Ye have seen what I did unto the Egyptians, *and how I bare you on eagles' wings*, and brought you unto myself."

The mountain appeared to be consumed by fire; the smoke was stifling. When the earth trembled and an earthquake seemed to be imminent, the watching tribes of Israel were terrified. They stared at their leader Moses who, unconcerned, was climbing into the mountain to meet Jehovah. Perfect love had cast out any fear which might have been in his soul. He was an ambassador, an intercessor, an official interpreter between God and men. Majestic and serene, he stood before the Lord and heard, "Now therefore, if ye will obey my voice indeed, and keep my covenant, then ye shall be a peculiar treasure unto me above all people: for all the earth is mine" (Ex. 19:5). Moses was overwhelmed with pride and humility. It was unbelievable that God had permitted this interview, for no man could be worthy of such favor. He remembered what the Lord had said: "I bare you on eagles' wings, and brought you unto myself." He considered the new promise, "If ye will obey my voice and keep my covenant, then shall ye be a peculiar treasure unto me above all people." The Almighty had *carried* them; now He was *conversing* with them, but greatest of all, Jehovah was making a *covenant* concerning their future. God's kindness would continue to support them; they were of incalculable worth. How could the Lord be so wonderful?

When the patriarch remembered what had been done for Israel, he was intensely grateful. The people had been slaves for four centuries and were completely impoverished. None of the men had received military training, and few, if any, possessed weapons. How could it be possible to wage war against hostile people and win?

The tribes were an unorganized multitude with no knowledge of how to survive in a wilderness. They had only the food brought from Egypt, and water was exceptionally scarce. Their problems were immense and complaints innumerable. The entire project of escaping to a better land seemed to be ridiculous.

Moses considered all that had happened and knew God had borne the people on eagles' wings and had provided everything necessary for survival. Eternal strength had been made perfect in human weakness. As the majestic bird of the heavens was said to carry its young on powerful, supporting wings, so the Almighty had supported His dependent children. The tribes were weak and unworthy, but they belonged to God as the eaglets did to their parents. Neither could fail their trusting offspring.

God's Unceasing Concern . . . *Awesome* (Deut. 32:11)

Moses was about to deliver his final message to Israel. He had considered the habits of the eagles. The words with which this study commenced were written on his heart. He remembered Jacob and said, "He found him in a desert land, and in the waste howling wilderness; he led him about, he instructed him, he kept him as the apple of his eye. As an eagle stirreth up her nest, fluttereth over her young, spreadeth abroad her wings, taketh them, beareth them on her wings: So the Lord alone did lead him, *and there was no strange god with him*" (Deut. 32:10–12). Thus Moses referred to the ancestor from whom the tribes of Israel descended. The personal history of the revered patriarch had been reproduced in the tribes. Throughout their journeys in the wilderness they were preserved by Jehovah, who had protected His children as the eagle did her offspring. There are five divisions which promote an understanding of the text.

(1) *How Strange are the Ways of God—"As an eagle stirreth up her nest."* Sometimes God appeared to be unkind when trying to help His people. Unless the parent eagle destroyed its nest, the young might remain there forever and would never fly. Even human babies cannot live forever encircled by a mother's arms. They need to be taught to walk, talk, and mature.

(2) *How Watchful are the Eyes of God—"fluttereth over her young."* The eagle stays close to her babies to attend to their every need. When the prophet Hannani spoke to King Asa, he said, "For the eyes of the Lord run to and fro throughout the whole earth, to

42

shew himself strong in the behalf of them whose heart is perfect toward him" (2 Chron. 16:9). A similar idea was expressed by David when he wrote: "The angel of the Lord encampeth round about them that fear him, and delivereth them" (Ps. 34:7). Whether it is believed or not, God is always close to His children.

(3) *How Strong are the Arms of God—"spreadeth abroad her wings."* The frantic movements made by the falling eaglet supplied the first lesson in how to fly. The gravitational pull was thwarted and overcome as the young bird began to exercise its inherent gift. Yet, while all this was taking place, the parent bird watched and was ready to catch her baby on strong supporting wings. Throughout every emergency, whether in or out of the nest, she was equal to each demand made upon her.

(4) *How Decisive are the Intentions of God—"taketh her young."* The young birds could never understand the motives of their mother. Inexperienced, they would interpret her behavior as thoughtless, irresponsible, and unkind. Job might have asked in adversity, "Why did God allow this to happen to me?" The eagle knows how to teach her young to fly, and without her expertise, disaster would destroy the family. Similarly, the Lord knows how to protect His children, and this was reflected in the Lord's prayer when He said, "Those that thou gavest me, I have kept" (John 17:12).

(5) *How Sufficient is the Provision of God—"beareth them on her wings."* Unlike the cuckoo, which has no affection for its young and deposits an egg in a borrowed nest, the eagle is watchful and protective. When necessity demands action, the bird responds. When danger threatens, the wings of the parent bird become a place of refuge. Like Jehovah, the bird might delay her rescue efforts, but she is never too late to help her endangered offspring. When the patriarchs considered these facts, it was easy to understand the sermon in the sky. The Lord's handiwork in creation revealed wisdom, majesty, and compassion. The same fact was emphasized by the Savior who said a falling sparrow was always seen by the watchful eyes of its Creator (see Matt. 10:29).

God's Unchanging Condition . . . *Admirable* (Isaiah 40:31)

"But they that wait upon the Lord shall renew their strength; they shall mount up with wings as eagles; they shall run and not be weary; and they shall walk, and not faint." Many years had passed, but even in a changing world, some things remained unaltered. Eagles continued to

nest in Israel's mountains and were watched by the prophet Isaiah. He was aware of the difficulties confronting his nation and realized the citizens of Israel were discouraged. He asked them a very important question. "Hast thou not known? hast thou not heard, that the everlasting God, the LORD, the Creator of the ends of the earth, fainteth not, neither is weary? There is no searching of his understanding. He giveth power to the faint, and to them that have no might he increaseth strength. Even the youths shall faint and be weary, and the young men shall utterly fall: *But they that wait upon the Lord shall renew their strength, they shall mount up with wings as eagles*" (Isa. 40:28–31).

Evidently the prophet had watched those powerful birds flying above the hills. Their majestic wings used every current of air and storms as means by which to fly higher. Isaiah suggested to his listeners that if God could impart such wisdom and strength to birds, He could give similar understanding to men and women. His utterances proved to be fascinating to people of all ages; His reasoning was challenging. He spoke of flying, running, walking, but people usually reverse that order. It is said that babies must crawl before they can walk and walk before they can run. Isaiah had other ways of explaining spiritual growth. "They that wait upon the Lord, shall renew their strength—*they shall mount up with wings as eagles.*" Excitement and compelling enthusiasm are evidence of spiritual awakening. Many young Christians become so energetic they try to change the world overnight. Nothing is impossible as they forge ahead with plans which sometimes are disastrous. The patience of God seems to say: "Give them time; they will descend from that lofty position and with a new purpose *will run and not be weary.*" Spiritual maturity is reached only when believers keep step with the Almighty—"they shall walk and not faint." When Enoch did that, he was ready to be taken into heaven.

Every child of God covets that capability. Unfortunately, some people are impatient and fail to wait for the Lord; others are discouraged and remain motionless when the Savior urges them to advance in faith. Blessed is the man who keeps step with his Maker. It is easy to hear His whispers when the believer and the Master walk side by side. The poet wrote:

> I tell Him all my sorrows;
> I tell Him all my joys:
> I tell Him all that pleases me;
> I tell Him what annoys.

He tells me what I ought to do;
He shows me how to try:
And so we walk together,
My Lord and I.

God's Unheeded Caution . . . *Awful* (Jeremiah 49:16)

The prophet Jeremiah had great reasons for denouncing the nations that were a constant menace to the Hebrews. They lived in a city which is now called Petra, where caves in the lofty hills were compared to the nests of eagles. The prophet said to those arrogant aggressors, "Thy terribleness hath deceived thee, and the pride of thine heart, O thou that dwellest in the clefts of the rock, that holdest the height of the hill; though thou shouldest make thy nest *as high as the eagle*, I will bring thee down from thence, saith the LORD."

Today that city that was carved out of the red cliffs by the Nabatean people is a solemn reminder of the veracity of God's words. Petra was impregnable; access was only gained through a narrow split in the earth where one man could hold the pass against an army. During the ministry of the minor prophets, the Edomites lived in caves high in the formidable hills, and the rocky fortress produced a sense of invincibility. The defiant people laughed when they heard the warnings of the prophets. They forgot that Jehovah who held earthquakes in His hand could easily shake them from their impregnable stronghold. Many years later when caravans and cameleers decided to bypass the city, Petra died for want of commerce, and its inhabitants disappeared among the nomads of the desert. Today the king of Jordan, assisted by international organizations, is planning to make the place one of the world's greatest tourist attractions.

The eagle is now considered to be an endangered species. Hunters frequently killed these wonderful birds to retain them as trophies, but that practice is no longer permitted. If the feathered monarch of the sky should ever become extinct, mankind would lose one of the greatest examples of the Creator's skill.

"And they appointed Kedesh in Galilee . . . and Shechem in mount Ephraim . . . and Hebron in the mountain of Judah. . . . And on the other side Jordan by Jericho eastward . . . Bezer in the wilderness . . . and Ramoth in Gilead . . . and Golan in Bashan" (Josh. 20:7–8).

Among the cities of Israel six were unique. They were specially selected to become havens of refuge for those whose lives were threatened. All were strategically situated; three were on the west side of the river Jordan and three on the east. They belonged to the tribe of Levi and each had its resident priest. Access was obtainable night or day, for the gates were never closed. According to Israel's legal system, when a person was inadvertently killed, his relatives were permitted to avenge the death of the deceased. The law supported the idea of an eye for an eye and a tooth for a tooth, and a person accused of murder was in great danger, even when the death had been accidental.

This procedure seemed to be unjust, and to rectify the situation six cities were chosen to become havens of refuge where those endangered could seek the protection of God and His priest. The accused was required to remain until his case could be examined by the "congregation" (city council), or until the priest died. Afterward, if he were innocent, he was permitted to return to his family.

Bible students believe this provision was a foreshadowing of the Savior, who was to become a refuge for sinners. God predicted, "And a man shall be as an hiding place from the wind, and a covert from the tempest; as rivers of water in a dry place, as the shadow of a great rock in a weary land" (Isa. 32:2). David expressed a similar thought when he wrote, "God is our refuge and strength, a very present help in trouble" (Ps. 46:1). An illuminating statement was made by the writer to the Hebrews, who said, "That by two immutable things, in which it was impossible for God to lie, we might have a strong consolation, *who have fled for refuge* to lay hold upon the hope set before us" (Heb. 6:18). After hiding from a storm in Somerset, England, the poet Toplady wrote:

> Oh, safe to the Rock that is higher than I
> My soul in its sorrows and conflicts would fly:
> So sinful, so weary, thine, thine would I be,
> Thou blest Rock of Ages, I'm hiding in Thee.

Many of the names found in the Bible are of great interest, but none are more attractive than those given to the cities of refuge. The Promised Land was not a large country, but God chose those remarkable centers so that in emergencies there was always one city within easy reach. It would be interesting to know whether God deliberately named those places. The cities of refuge were called Kedesh, Shechem, Hebron, Bezer, Ramoth, and Golan, but each name had a special meaning. If they were meant to reveal attributes of the Savior, the list becomes exceptionally interesting.

Kedesh—(The Sanctuary) . . . *A Refuge for the Unholy*

It is fitting that this should be the first of the cities mentioned; it means *the sanctuary*, and no person could enter the house of God without seeing the altar! This was the dwelling place of the Almighty who was the personification of purity and holiness. When God descended upon mount Sinai, the people of Israel were forbidden to touch the sacred hill. It was astonishing when God revealed a way sinners could enter into His presence and be sure of His protection. There was an outstanding difference between the Old Testament refuge and that supplied through the redeeming death of God's Son. The offenders who fled to Kedesh were only guilty of an accidental death, a regrettable occurrence for which they could not be blamed. People who were criminals, who had deliberately committed murder, were not welcomed in any city of refuge. When God through His grace supplied redemption for mankind, limitations were removed.

> The vilest offender who truly believes;
> That moment from Jesus a pardon receives.

When Paul wrote to Timothy, he said, "For there is one God, and one mediator between God and men, the man Christ Jesus" (1 Tim. 2:5). The apostle John wrote the words of the Lord, "I Jesus have sent mine angel to testify unto you these things in the churches. I am the root and the offspring of David, and the bright and morning star. And the Spirit and the bride say, Come. And let him that heareth say, Come. And let him that is athirst come. And whosoever will, let him take of the water of life freely" (Rev. 22:16–17). The welcome given by the Savior supersedes all others. Our High Priest, unlike those of the Jewish world, will never die. When He offers sanctuary, it is limitless.

47

Shechem—(The Shoulder) . . . *A Refuge for the Unsure*

Archeologists have uncovered evidence which proves the ancient city of Shechem was protected by massive fortifications. Its inhabitants controlled most of the trade routes of northern Canaan, and it is believed the name related to strength. Even in modern times women carry water pots on their shoulder. God said of His servant, Eliakim, "And the key of the house of David will I lay upon his shoulder; so he shall open, and none shall shut; and he shall shut, and none shall open" (Isa. 22:22). The same prophet wrote of the Messiah, "For unto us a child is born, unto us a son is given: and the government shall be upon his shoulder: and his name shall be called Wonderful, Counselor, The mighty God, The everlasting Father, The Prince of Peace" (Isa. 9:6). Shechem was a fortress in which people were secure. It was situated about thirty miles north of Jerusalem and could be reached easily by people in urgent need. It offered protection to the weak and confidence to the fearful.

It is interesting to remember that shepherds carried their weak or injured sheep on their shoulders. The strength of the men overshadowed the weakness of the animals. Alone and unaided the sheep were victims of predators, but upon the shoulder of its guardian, even the weakest lamb was safe. Men who distrusted their own capabilities looked at the fortifications of Shechem and were reassured that once inside, they would be safe. After many years the Lord Jesus came to earth and provided a greater refuge than had ever been known. He assured the disciples that His arms could protect them from all danger, even the gates of hell would not prevail against His kingdom. The text, "Be still and know that I am God," should strengthen every soul whose faith is in the Rock of Ages.

Hebron—(Fellowship) . . . *A Refuge for the Unwanted*

"These were the cities appointed for all the children of Israel, and for the stranger that sojourneth among them." The followers of Moses belonged to an exclusive society; foreigners were seldom welcomed unless they came to trade. The Hebrews believed they alone were the chosen of God, and people of other nations were constantly reminded of that fact. It was significant when God made provision to extend His grace to all nations. Was this a foreshadowing of the era when even Gentiles would cease to be strangers and become fellow heirs of the commonwealth of Israel? Paul wrote to the Christians in Ephesus saying, "Now therefore ye are no more strangers and foreigners, but fellowcitizens with the saints, and of the household of God" (Eph. 2:19). The entire district occupied by the people of Hebron was fertile and crops were plentiful. "A large number of springs and wells dot the landscape, making it certain of occupation. . . . Apple, plum, fig, pomegranate, apricot and nut trees are produced in abundance. Grapes, melons and several vegetables are produced in profusion from the rich soil of valley and terrace" (quoted from the *Zondervan Pictorial Encyclopedia of the Bible*, Vol. 3, p. 108). Hebron was a very wealthy and important place; there was sufficient of everything for its residents. It was a city of fellowship.

When considering this ancient place, it is wise to recall how the Savior said, "I am the bread of life: he that cometh to me shall never hunger; and he that believeth on me, shall never thirst" (John 6:35). Christ is truly Hebron for His people. He is pleased when people seek shelter within His embrace and enjoys communion with them. Unlike the Jehovah of Old Testament ages who was remote, mysterious, and sometimes forbidding, the Lord Jesus Christ lives within His people and appreciates their fellowship.

Bezer—(The Stronghold) . . . *A Refuge for the Unable*

Little is known of this city except for the fact that it was chosen by Moses to be one of the three cities of refuge on the east of Jordan. "Then Moses severed three cities on this side Jordan toward the sunrising; That the slayer might flee thither, which should kill his neighbor unawares, and hated him not in times past; and that fleeing unto one of these cities he might live: Namely, Bezer in the wilderness in the plain country, of the Reubenites; and Ramoth in Gilead, of the Gadites; and Golan in Bashan, of the Manassites" (Deut. 4:41–43).

It is generally accepted that this name means a stronghold, and this might imply that since it was built in the plain country, without it the inhabitants would have been defenseless. Apparently there were no mountains in the vicinity; everything was flat, and enemies could easily have conquered the people. This place of refuge was formidable, and any man who sought sanctuary within its walls was safe.

If this city were meant to be a type of Christ, then its message was unmistakable. The psalmist said, "Thou art my hiding place; thou shalt preserve me from trouble; thou shalt compass me about with songs of deliverance" (Ps. 32:7). David also said, "Thou art my hiding place and my shield: I hope in thy word" (Ps. 119:114). When Paul wrote to the Colossians he reminded them, "Your life is hid with Christ in God" (Col. 3:3). Throughout his lifetime David knew what it meant to be sheltered by Jehovah. He wrote, "For in the time of trouble he shall hide me in his pavilion" (Ps. 27:5). "The Lord is my strength and my shield; my heart trusted in him, and I am helped: therefore my heart greatly rejoiceth; and with my song will I praise him" (Ps. 28:7). A shield came between its owner and the aggressor; God is a shield to all who trust Him; He stands between the soul and the threatening enemy.

Ramoth—(Exalted: The High Place) . . . *A Refuge for the Unworthy*

This city was also called Ramoth-Gilead. A. R. Fausset says the name means "the heights of Gilead because it was a fortress commanding the countryside, and for which during history, the armies of Israel fought repeatedly." The fortress was upon high ground, and any man seeking refuge within the walls would need to turn his eyes heavenward and climb until he reached his desired haven.

It is never wise to read into a text something not there, but David said, "I will lift up mine eyes unto the hills, from whence cometh my help. My help cometh from the LORD, which made heaven and earth. He will not suffer thy foot to be moved: he that keepeth thee will not slumber. Behold, he that keepeth Israel shall neither slumber nor sleep. The Lord is thy keeper" (see Ps. 121:1–5). The refuge of every Christian is found in Christ. Luke described how Peter and the apostles addressed the council. "Then Peter and the other apostles answered and said, We ought to obey God rather than men. The God of our fathers raised up Jesus, whom ye slew and hanged on a tree. Him hath God exalted with his right hand to be a Prince and a Savior, for to give repentance to Israel, and forgiveness of sins" (Acts 5:29–31). The Lord is the High Priest of His people, and He said, "Him that cometh to me I will in no wise cast out" (John 6:37). The writer to the Hebrews said, "Let us therefore come boldly unto the throne of grace, that we may obtain mercy, and find grace to help in time of need" (Heb. 4:16).

Golan—(Exile or Separated) . . . *A Refuge for the Undesirable*

"They gave Golan in Bashan with her suburbs, to be a city of refuge for the slayer" (Josh. 21:27). It is said they sanctified or separated the cities; that is, they set them apart. The name might be interpreted as "a place for exiles; or for people unable to find refuge elsewhere." The crime of which they were accused and the possibility of involvement with bloodshed made the manslayers undesirable in most places in Israel. It may be a matter of conjecture whether this had any meaning for the untouchables who met the Savior. Matthew recorded a moment when this was vividly portrayed. "When he [Jesus] was come down from the mountain, great multitudes followed him, And, behold, there came a leper and worshiped him, saying, Lord, if thou wilt, thou canst make me clean. And Jesus put forth his hand and touched him, saying, I will; be thou clean. And immediately his leprosy was cleansed" (Matt. 8:1–3). All lepers were exiles in Israel; the presence of the dreaded disease expelled them from the presence of people. They were compelled to live in hovels away from centers of habitation, and even their food, if it were supplied by relatives, had to be left at an isolated place and collected later by the outcasts. Association with healthy people was strictly forbidden. There was no city of refuge to which a leper could flee; he had no hope of survival.

It was interesting that one of the six cities of refuge should be called "a city for exiles." Yet that was precisely what the manslayer became when a charge of murder was brought against him. Surviving members of the deceased man's family would insist on avenging the death of their loved one, and, apart from the cities of refuge, there were no hiding places in the nation. If the endangered man refused to avail himself of the offered salvation, he had no defense against his enemies. Abner, who was in that predicament, was only a step from safety, but he refused to move and died in the gateway of Hebron (2 Sam. 3:27). He did not consider it would have been better to live within the city than to be buried outside. The writer to the Hebrews asked a question for which there has never been an answer. "How shall we escape, if we neglect so great salvation?" (Heb. 2:3).

THE RETURN OF THE ARK—HOW TO
GET GOD BACK INTO OUR LIVES

"And it came to pass, while the ark abode in Kirjath-Jearim, that the time was long; for it was twenty years: and all the house of Israel lamented after the Lord" (1 Sam. 7:2).

Four chapters in the first book of Samuel express the history of the Hebrew nation. They begin with the name Ichabod, which was given to an infant son and meant "The Lord hath departed"; they end with the name Ebenezer, given when Israel seemed to have been reborn and God returned to dwell with His family. Together these chapters (1 Sam. 5–8) provide one of the most entrancing accounts in the Old Testament.

A Disturbing Regression . . . *Reproachable*

The children of Israel were desolate; their confidence had been shattered, their happiness ruined. They had been defeated in battle by the Philistines, and it was incomprehensible. "And when the people were come into the camp, the elders of Israel said, Wherefore hath the LORD smitten us to day before the Philistines? Let us fetch the ark of the covenant of the LORD out of Shiloh unto us, that, when it cometh among us, it may save us out of the hand of our enemies . . . And when the ark of the covenant of the LORD came into the camp, all Israel shouted with a great shout, so that the earth rang again" (1 Sam. 4:3–5).

Unfortunately the enthusiasm manifested by the Hebrews was false. The ark of the covenant was only a sacred symbol of the presence of Jehovah, but it almost became an idol. It was to be regretted that the warriors of the nation had more confidence in the ark than they had in the one it represented. The Jews were proud that God resided in their midst but were content that He should be secluded in the tabernacle at Shiloh. Jehovah was a desirable asset as long as He did not interfere with their likes and dislikes. They expected much from Him but gave little in return. When trouble overwhelmed the nation, they asked, "Wherefore hath the Lord smitten us today before the Philistines?" They saw no fault in themselves and in that respect resemble others who live today. When men and women are confronted by tragedy, their first reaction is to ask why the misfortune was permitted. How could God be so unkind?

52

A Dead Religion . . . *Regrettable*

During one awful day Israel lost a battle, saw the ark of God captured, their high priest fatally injured, and his daughter-in-law die in childbirth. The woman's heart was broken when she heard of the misfortunes of the nation. "And she named the child Ichabod, saying. The glory is departed from Israel; because the ark of God was taken, and because of her father in law, and her husband" (1 Sam. 4:21–22).

It should be remembered that the heathens believed the ark was God! "The Philistines were afraid, for they said, God is come into the camp. Woe unto us! . . . Who shall deliver us out of the hand of these mighty Gods? These are the Gods that smote the Egyptians with all the plagues in the wilderness" (1 Sam. 4:7–8). The Jews were very orthodox. Rituals were faithfully observed, but their religion was dead. They exhibited a form of godliness but were bereft of spiritual power. The adjacent nations were idolaters; the children of Israel were legalists. The message sent by Christ to the church at Sardis might have been applicable to the ancient Hebrews. "Thou hast a name, that thou livest, and art dead" (Rev. 3:1). It was pathetic that after the ark had been returned by the Philistines, it was permitted to remain at Kirjath-Jearim for twenty years. The people had a God whose presence was never enjoyed.

The nation observed its festivals, offered sacrifices, and donated money for the upkeep of their sanctuary, but true prophets were hard to find. It was necessary to get God back into the life of the nation. Throughout the world people recognize that something has gone wrong with the church. There is money to finance projects; beautiful buildings are being erected in countless areas, and yet the advice of the people of God is seldom sought. Television programs bring into homes scenes and language that should be intolerable, and many who were leaders in Christian communities have lost their fervor. The church does not need new interpretations of truth; its members require fresh experiences of the presence and power of God.

A Definite Request . . . *Reasonable*

The prophet Samuel knew how to bring God back into the life of the nation, but even he could do nothing until "Israel lamented after the Lord." It was only after the nation repented of its sin that a spiritual awakening became possible. When this happened in Israel,

"Samuel spake unto all the house of Israel, saying, If ye do return unto the LORD with all your hearts, then put away the strange gods and Ashtaroth from among you, and prepare your hearts unto the LORD, and serve him only: and he will deliver you out of the hand of the Philistines" (1 Sam. 7:3). That promise was repeated to Solomon. "If my people, which are called by my name, shall humble themselves, and pray, and seek my face, and turn from their wicked ways; then will I hear from heaven, and will forgive their sin, and will heal their land" (2 Chron. 7:14). Elijah insisted on the destruction of idolatry and was not content until those who had ruined the nation were removed permanently (see 1 Kings 18:40). God never asks His people to do the impossible unless He supplies the strength to do what is necessary. The people who had made idols were asked to destroy them, but sometimes they were reluctant to obey God's command. "In the seventh year of Jehu . . . Jehoash did that which was right in the sight of the Lord all his days wherein Jehoiada the priest instructed him. *But the high places were not taken away:* the people still sacrificed and burnt incense in the high places" (2 Kings 12:1–3). Jeroboam encouraged idolatry because he was afraid worshiping in Jerusalem might undermine his own popularity (see 1 Kings 12:26–31). The rich young ruler who asked the Lord about eternal life evidently desired wealth and refused to abandon his idol.

> The dearest idol I have known;
> What e're that idol be:
> Help me to tear it from its throne,
> And worship only Thee.

Separation from sin is the forerunner of successful service. The Lord emphasized that truth when He said, "No man can serve two masters: for either he will hate the one, and love the other, or else he will hold to the one, and despise the other. Ye cannot serve God and mammon" (Matt. 6:24). Lot was asked to choose between the plains of Sodom and the hills of God; the prodigal son was required to choose between his father's embrace and the companions who nearly destroyed his soul. Joshua said, "Choose you this day whom ye will serve . . . but as for me and my house, we will serve the Lord" (Josh. 24:15).

A Delightful Result . . . *Remarkable*

"And the children of Israel said unto Samuel, Cease not to cry unto the LORD our God for us, that he will save us out of the hand of the Philistines. And Samuel took a sucking lamb, and offered it for a burnt offering wholly unto the LORD: And Samuel cried unto the LORD for Israel; and the LORD heard him. And as Samuel was offering up the burnt offering, the Philistines drew near to battle against Israel: but the LORD thundered with a great thunder on that day upon the Philistines, and discomforted them; and they were smitten before Israel. . . . Then Samuel took a stone, and set it between Mizpeh and Shen, and called the name of it, Ebenezer, saying, Hitherto hath the LORD helped us" (1 Sam. 7:8–12). Israel's thrilling victory may be considered under four headings.

(1) *The Glorious Supplication . . . Asking.* "Cease not to cry unto the Lord our God for us." A man is never closer to heaven than when he kneels to pray. "The effectual fervent prayer of a righteous man availeth much" (James 5:16). A church that never *prays* is only a charitable institution.

(2) *A Gracious Sacrifice . . . Atoning.* "And Samuel took a sucking lamb, and offered it for a burnt offering wholly unto the LORD." The Bible says, "Without shedding of blood is no remission . . ." (Heb. 9:22). God commanded the deliverance from Egypt should never be forgotten, and parents were told to explain to their children the meaning of the Passover Feast. The death of the lamb was the only basis upon which fellowship with the Almighty became possible. True life begins in the shadow of Christ's cross.

(3) *A Gigantic Storm . . . Advancing.* "And as Samuel was offering up the burnt offering, the Philistines drew near to battle against Israel: but the LORD thundered with a great thunder on that day upon the Philistines, and discomforted them" (1 Sam. 7:10). Anything is possible when a sincere soul stands humbly before his Maker. A display of God's awesome artillery can terrorize His enemies. During the life of Elijah, God used the clouds to bring rain; in this instance He used a storm to protect His people.

(4) *A Great Stone . . . Announcing.* "Then Samuel took a stone, and set it up between Mizpeh and Shen, and called the name of it, Ebenezer, saying, Hitherto hath the Lord helped us." True gratitude begets praise. The memorial pillar reminded every traveler of God's faithfulness. It was significant that "the Philistines were subdued, and they came no more into the coast of Israel; and the hand of the LORD was against the Philistines all the days of Samuel" (1 Sam. 7:13). The presence and prayers of a dedicated man can be of inestimable worth when God's people are in danger. Life be-

gins—and it can end, in the shadow of the Cross of Christ. Everything depends upon the choice of the person who stands there.

Aleksandr Solzhenitsyn, the famous author who was imprisoned by the Russian government, tells of an experience when he was overwhelmed by despondency. He was digging near his prison camp when he realized the hopelessness of his plight. The communists appeared to be invincible; it was foolish to resist! He knew that if he quit his job he would be killed by the guards as an example to all other dissidents, but he did not care. It would be better to die than to live as a slave. He left his job and went to sit on a nearby bench. He had seen what happened to others who had acted similarly, but he was prepared to suffer the same fate.

Suddenly, he sensed a presence and, looking up, saw an old man whose eyes were without expression. As he watched, the stranger drew a cross in the dirt and, without saying a word, went back to his task. Solzhenitzyn stared at it and realized goodness always outlasts evil. Oppression appeared to be invincible, but the cause of Christ and freedom would ultimately triumph. As new hope filled his soul, he rejoined the other prisoners. Today the writings of that great man influence the nations of the world. It might be wrong to suggest God came back to him; probably, the Lord had never left!

> The Cross, it standeth fast
> Defying every blast.
> The winds of hell have blown;
> The world, its hate hath shown;
> Yet it is not overthrown,
> Hallelujah for the Cross.
>
> Horatius Bonar

THE HUNGRY MOTHER WHO COULD NOT FORGET

"And it came to pass after these things, that the son of the woman, the mistress of the house, fell sick; and his sickness was so sore, that there was no breath left in him. And she said unto Elijah, What have I to do with thee, O man of God? art thou come unto me to call my sin to remembrance, and to slay my son? (1 Kings 17:17–18).

This story begins with one of the most pathetic scenes described in the Old Testament. A lonely, despairing woman stood before her small son and sorrowfully made a tragic decision. The boy was hungry, but she had very little food to offer him. With great care she had handled the supplies that were left, and it is safe to assume the lad was given most of what had been available. Fearfully, she saw her resources dwindling, and finally the dreaded moment arrived. She only possessed "an handful of meal in a barrel, and a little oil in a cruse" (1 Kings 17:12).

A small cake might be made and baked, but afterward she and her son would die. A terrible drought had ruined the economy of the city. Three years had elapsed since the heavens produced rain; animals had perished, and many people had left in search of better conditions. The woman had no helper; her husband had died, and she had been left with the responsibility of maintaining a home for her child. The position was extremely critical, the outlook bleak! Leaving the boy in the home, she went to collect sticks for a fire and saw a traveler entering the city. "Poor man; he also would be hungry, but if he came to Zarephath in search of food he had made a great mistake." Perhaps they passed the time of day, then she proceeded with her task.

The ancient writer said, "And when he [Elijah] came to the gate of the city, behold, the widow woman was there gathering of sticks: and he called to her, and said, Fetch me, I pray thee, a little water in a vessel, that I may drink. And as she was going to fetch it, he called to her, and said, Bring me, I pray thee, a morsel of bread in thine hand. And she said, As the LORD thy God liveth, I have not a cake, but an handful of meal in a barrel, and a little oil in a cruse: and behold, I am gathering two sticks, that I may go in and dress it for me and my son, that we may eat it, and die. And Elijah said unto her: Fear not; go and do as thou hast said: but make me thereof a little cake first, and bring it unto me, and after make for thee and for thy son. For thus saith the Lord God of Israel, The barrel of meal shall not waste, neither shall the cruse of oil fail, until the day that the LORD sendeth rain upon the earth" (1 Kings 17:10–14).

The Disturbing Past . . . *Grace Watching*

It would be informative to know the details of this woman's life. The Scripture suggests her career had been difficult. When her child died, she asked the prophet, "Art thou come unto me to call my sin to remembrance, and to slay my son?" (1 Kings 17:18). The sin of which she felt guilty remains unknown, but in her mind the distracted mother associated it with her boy. Her transgression might have been any kind of inadvisable conduct, but she interpreted her misfortune as being retribution for evil conduct. Maybe she had been engaged in premarital folly, and, as was the case with David and Bathsheba, the child conceived out of wedlock died as evidence of God's displeasure. When this woman considered her indiscretion, the tormented mother believed she was responsible for the lad's death.

There appears to have been some happiness in her earlier years; she had married and given birth to a child. Then her joy had been overshadowed by the death of her husband, and perhaps she considered herself to blame for his death. The old saying "When it rains, it pours," had been true in her life. As though that were not enough, the paralyzing famine diminished the supply of food, and she and her son were starving to death. Even the bravest of saints would be troubled by such conditions. Her disturbing past refused to disappear, but through those distressing events God's grace was working on her behalf.

The widow of Zarephath had probably heard of Elijah, but the possibility of their meeting was very remote. Yet, he knew about her and believed she would become a part of his life. The Bible says: "And the word of the LORD came unto him, saying, Arise, get thee to Zarephath, which belongeth to Zidon, and dwell there: behold, I have commanded a widow woman there to sustain thee" (1 Kings 17:8–9). Probably God never audibly addressed the lady, for she expressed surprise when the stranger requested food. The text may mean God made arrangements for the woman to assist the prophet. The writer to the Hebrews referred to the angels as being "ministering spirits, sent forth to minister for them who shall be heirs of salvation" (Heb. 1:14). Perhaps the Lord instructed His angelic messengers to supervise the operation in Zarephath, and although the distraught mother believed she was alone, her future was secure in the hands of God.

David also expressed that fact when he exclaimed, "Why art thou cast down, O my soul? and why art thou disquieted within me? Hope thou in God: for I shall yet praise him for the help of his countenance" (Ps. 42:5). Someone has said, "Affliction is the Good Shepherd's *black dog,*" and the animal is never far from its owner. The grace of God is constantly attentive to the needs of His children.

The Daily Provision . . . *Grace Working*

"And the barrel of meal wasted not, neither did the cruse of oil fail, according to the word of the LORD, which he spake by Elijah" (1 Kings 17:16). It seems evident that since Zarephath was about one hundred miles from the main centers of Israel, its water supply was not as critical. Maybe the snows of Lebanon eased the situation, for at the time of Elijah's arrival the woman still possessed a small quantity. That she was willing to share it with a stranger was not surprising. Mr. Porter, in the *Pulpit Commentary* (vol. 5, p. 385), says, "The gift of water to the thirsty is always regarded as a sacred duty in the East. Never, during many years of residence in Syria, and many a long day's travel, have I been refused a draught of water by a single individual of any sect or race. The Bedawy in the desert has shared with me the last drop in his water skin."

The prophet's request for food was more startling. His insistence that a cake be baked for him *first*, should remind everybody of the words of Jesus, "But seek ye first the kingdom of God, and his righteousness; and all these things shall be added unto you" (Matt. 6:33). The promise that the supply of food would not diminish removed her fear. "And she went and did according to the saying of Elijah: and she, and he, and her house, did eat many days" (*a full year* [marginal reading]) (1 Kings 17:15).

Dr. W. H. Thomson, writing about the home of the widow, says, "Our translation makes Elijah live in a loft, but it is not very accurate. The word in Hebrew is *'alliyeh'*, and this is a common Arabic word for the upper rooms of houses. This 'alliyeh' is the most desirable part of the establishment, is best fitted up, and is still given to guests who are to be treated with honor. The women and servants live below, and their apartment is called *ardiyeh* or ground floor. . . .

The poorer people have no 'alliyeh'. We may infer several things from this word: that the mode of building in Elijah's time, and the custom of giving the 'alliyeh' to the guest, were the same as now. This woman was not originally among the very poorest classes, but her extreme destitution was owing to the desperate famine which then prevailed. The little chamber made for Elisha by the Shunammite is also called 'alliyeh,' and was therefore an upper room, respectable and comfortable. They are more retired than the apartments of the house, and, of course, appropriate for the resting place of prophets" [W. M. Thomson, *The Land and the Book* (London: Thomas Nelson and Sons, 1910), p. 139].

Each day throughout the year the woman knew God's servant lived upstairs and his presence sanctified every meal. When she prepared the food, she was aware of the miracle being performed daily. Jehovah was sustaining His servant, and she and her boy were receiving the overflow of God's provision. It was impossible to live in the presence of the Lord and starve to death! She would have appreciated the hymn, "Great is Thy faithfulness, O God my Father."

The Desperate Plea . . . *Grace Waiting*

"And it came to pass after these things, that the son of the woman, the mistress of the house, fell sick; and his sickness was so sore, that there was no breath left in him. And she said unto Elijah, What have I to do with thee, O thou man of God? art thou come unto me to call my sin to remembrance, and to slay my son?" (1 Kings 17:17–18).

The widow of Zarephath resembled all women. It would be difficult to decide which was her greater need—food for her body or peace for her mind. During earlier years she had committed an unidentified sin, and although God had pardoned her, she could not forgive herself! Each time trouble devastated her life she believed it was a punishment from God. Her vision of Jehovah was biased; she did not realize that when God forgives sin, He forgets it! The Lord, through His servant Jeremiah, said, "I will forgive their iniquity, and I will remember their sin no more" (Jer. 31:34). His grace and kindness are beyond measurement; His love supersedes anything known to man.

The mother in Zarephath did not understand this fact; she believed God would always remember her evil deed. The Lord was filled with compassion and proceeded to perform a different kind of miracle. Her child became ill and died, and immediately the distracted mother believed the tragedy to be additional evidence that God was relentless. Her mind became a prey to fear; she was haunted by memories.

With infinite pity God watched her and devised a way by which her fear would be removed forever. The woman was about to learn a truth that Paul taught centuries later. "And we know that all things work together for good to them that love God, to them who are the called according to his purpose" (Rom. 8:28). "And he [Elijah] said unto her, Give me thy son. And he took him out of her bosom, and carried him up into a loft, where he abode, and laid him upon his own bed. And he cried unto the LORD. . . . And the LORD heard the voice of Elijah, and the soul of the child came into him again, and he revived. And Elijah took the child . . . and delivered him unto his mother . . ." (1 Kings 17:19–23).

That glorious miracle not only revealed the power and majesty of the Almighty; it helped the woman to understand God's grace was greater than her guilt. What she considered to be an act of vengeance was a channel through which the Lord sent His benediction. That revelation produced greater happiness than she had ever known. It was wonderful to see and hold her boy, but even greater to imagine a smile upon the face of her heavenly Father.

The Delightful Peace . . . *Grace Whispering*

"And the woman said to Elijah, Now by this I know that thou art a man of God, and that the word of the LORD in thy mouth is truth" (1 Kings 17:24). Most of the theologians believe "the prophet spent about one year in the Wady Cherith, and two and a half years in the house of the widow" (*Pulpit Commentary*, vol. 5, p. 417). Thus did Jehovah hide His servant from the search parties of King Ahab and at the same time provide food and fellowship for the woman and her child. It must be concluded that however wonderful the fellowship of birds in the hills, the affection of the small family was more desirable. The grateful mother discovered a new basis upon which to rest her faith. She said to the prophet, "*I know* the word of the Lord in thy mouth is truth." If she were ever tempted to worry about her former failure, the word of Elijah dispelled her fears and removed her doubts. When she listened to the counsel of the man of God, she became aware of the whispers of another voice—a still small voice—which brought increasing peace to her soul. She began to understand that if God were not merciful, no one would enter His kingdom.

A troubled conscience is a most aggravating companion; it is a thorn in the flesh which destroys the relationship between God and His children. Even the apostle Paul was troubled when he remembered how he persecuted the early Christians and consented to the death of Stephen. Nevertheless, he found comfort in the truth expressed in the letter to the Hebrews, "For if the blood of bulls and of goats, and the ashes of an heifer sprinkling the unclean, sanctifieth to the purifying of the flesh: How much more shall the blood of Christ, who through the eternal Spirit offered himself without spot to God, *purge your conscience* from dead works to serve the living God?" (Heb. 9:13–14).

An Indian, trying to describe a troubled conscience, said, "Conscience is a three cornered object in my heart. It remains still when I am good, but when I do something evil, it turns around and around, and the corners hurt a lot. If I continue to do evil, the corners wear off, and it does not hurt any more" (quoted from *The Construction Digest*).

"And he [Elisha] said, Thus saith the LORD, *Make this valley full of ditches. For thus saith the* LORD, *Ye shall not see wind, neither shall ye see rain; yet that valley shall be filled with water, that ye may drink, both ye, and your cattle, and your beasts . . . And it came to pass in the morning, when the meat offering was offered, that, behold, there came water by the way of Edom, and the country was filled with water" (2 Kings 3:16–17, 20).*

During prolonged droughts in southern Africa, the need for water becomes acute, and periodically farmers convene special meetings in which to pray for rain. Sandy river beds provide playgrounds for children and ideal sites for picnics. A friend explained to me how he nearly lost his life on such an outing. The family was about to enjoy a meal when they heard a roaring sound coming from the direction of the mountains. Quickly they climbed to the top of the river banks, but they were only just in time, for a wall of water rushed down the arid bed sweeping away a phonograph, baby carriage, and their picnic baskets and food. A storm in the distant mountains had sent torrents of water rushing down the river bed, and if they had not responded immediately to the warning given by the father, all would have drowned. Yet, so my friend informed me, within an hour the water had disappeared, and calm was restored to the area.

Thousands of years ago in Israel a similar thing happened, but unfortunately, the account remains an unfamiliar story within the Scriptures. During the reign of Ahab, the king of Moab had been compelled to pay an enormous tribute to his conqueror. This meant a considerable loss to the nation's resources, for annually the king forfeited 100,000 lambs and 100,000 unshorn rams. After the death of Ahab when Jehoram succeeded his father, Mesha the king of Moab refused to continue the annual payment, and this aroused the anger of Israel's king. Believing help was needed to overcome the reluctant enemy, he sought assistance from the kings of Judah and Edom, and together they planned to subdue the rebellion. Unfortunately, they approached through the desert, and according to Josephus, when their guide took the wrong route in the wilderness, the united forces were soon in jeopardy. Their thirst became so intense, it was feared the men would die in the desert. It was that possibility that made the king of Israel exclaim, "Alas, that the LORD hath called these three kings together, to deliver them into the hand of Moab! But Jehoshaphat (the king of Judah) said, Is there not here a prophet of the LORD, that we may inquire of the LORD by him? And one of the king of Israel's servants answered and said, Here is Elisha the son of Shaphat, which poured water on the hands of Elijah. . . . So the king of Israel and Jehoshaphat and the king of Edom went down to him" (2 Kings 3:10–12).

The Peace of God . . . *How Achievable*

"And Elisha said, As the LORD of hosts liveth, before whom I stand, surely, were it not that I regard the presence of Jehoshaphat the king of Judah, I would not look toward thee, nor see thee. But now bring me a minstrel. And it came to pass, when the minstrel played, that the hand of the LORD came upon him" (2 Kings 3:14–15). Evidently Elisha was upset as he contemplated the evil that had been wrought by the family of Ahab. He detested everything that the king represented, and even as he looked at the hypocritical ruler, his soul was filled with disgust. Apparently the prophet realized he was not in the right mood to listen to the whispers of God. The Lord said to David, "Be still, and know that I am God" (Ps. 46:10). The prophet Elisha appreciated the same message. How could he or anyone else listen to the voice of the Almighty when his soul was disturbed? He called for a minstrel and listened to the haunting melodies of the musician. Slowly, peace and tranquility were restored, and as the realization of the divine presence thrilled his heart, the prophet delivered his message.

Earth-born clouds that eclipse the Sun of Righteousness are a menace. Even when anger seems to be justified, anything that destroys the sanctity of the human temple must be regarded as dangerous. Cleland B. McAfee was correct when he wrote:

> There is a place of quiet rest,
> Near to the heart of God,
> A place where sin cannot molest,
> Near to the heart of God.
>
> O Jesus, blest Redeemer,
> Sent from the heart of God,
> Hold us who wait before Thee,
> Near to the heart of God.

Sometimes people permit circumstances to destroy their serenity; they act hastily and say and do things not reflecting the majesty of God.

I remember occasions when annoyance appeared to demand a certain course of action, when my mother said, "Son, sleep on it; you will be more able to handle the matter in the morning." She was always correct, and I would have been wise had I followed her advice more often. Sometimes I became irritable and impetuously desired retaliation. The words of John Whittier were God's minstrel in my life.

> Drop Thy still dews of quietness,
> 'Till all our strivings cease:
> Take from our souls the strain and stress
> And let our ordered lives confess,
> The beauty of Thy peace.
>
> Breathe through the heats of our desire
> Thy coolness and Thy balm,
> Let sense be dumb, Let flesh retire,
> Speak through the earthquake, wind, and fire
> O still small voice of calm.

The Promise of God . . . *How Assuring*

"And he [Elisha] said, Thus saith the LORD, Make this valley full of ditches. For thus saith the LORD, Ye shall not see wind, neither shall ye see rain; yet that valley shall be filled with water, that ye may drink, both ye, and your cattle, and your beasts" (2 Kings 3:16–17).

When Elisha continued his message saying, "And this is but a light thing in the sight of the LORD: he will deliver the Moabites also into your hand" (2 Kings 3:18), Jehoshaphat the king of Judah rejoiced and believed God's promise. The soldiers of the three armies began to dig in the dry watercourse, and the entire landscape was quickly changed. Possibly those men were obeying orders. There is no evidence that they believed what Elisha had promised. Perhaps they thought it was better to work than to stand around doing nothing. The faith of Jehoshaphat was remarkable, for although there were no signs of an approaching storm, he believed water would be forthcoming. Long afterward the writer to the Hebrews wrote, "Now faith is the substance of things hoped for, the evidence of things not seen" (Heb. 11:1). That fact was clearly expressed in the attitude of the king of Judah.

Perhaps the kings of Israel and Edom scoffed, for the cloudless skies seemed to mock their efforts. It was extremely unlikely that help would be forthcoming. The promise of the prophet appeared to be ludicrous. Elisha's faith was evident; he was assured that nothing was too hard for Jehovah to accomplish. It is not known how the many soldiers found implements with which to dig. If their equipment included small shovels, their task would have been simplified. If not, they improvised or used their hands to dig the ditches in the sand. Their efforts provided the strangest scene mentioned in the Bible. When they realized their existence depended upon the prophet whose commands they were obeying, their objections were silenced. Finally their task was completed; mounds of earth were everywhere, and the river bed was filled with innumerable ditches.

The Plan of God . . . *How Accurate*

"And it came to pass in the morning, when the meat offering was offered, that, behold, there came water by the way of Edom, and the country was filled with water" (2 Kings 3:20). Josephus, the Jewish historian, said, "When the prophet had said this, the next day, before the sunrising, a great torrent ran strongly; for God had caused it to rain very plentifully at the distance of three days journey into Edom, so that the army and the cattle found water to drink in abundance" (*Antiquities* 9.3.2). It remains unclear what Josephus meant when he said the storm burst at a distance of three days into Edom. That distance would not be great for a man to walk, but if Josephus meant a three-day camel ride, the storm could have been located much farther away. The matter is of small importance, for it was the time of the arrival of the water that was impressive.

God had instructed Israel to offer two lambs every day, one in the morning, the other in the evening (see Ex. 29:38–42). It was significant that in spite of their acute thirst and the continuation of their problems, the people did not forget to honor the Lord and observe His commandments. It might have been easy to believe He had forsaken His people, but whatever the circumstances seemed to suggest, the priests proceeded to observe the commandments of God, and as they did, the water reached the camp. Many years later, the Savior said, "Seek ye first the kingdom of God, and his righteousness; and all these things shall be added unto you" (Matt. 6:33). God's timing was perfect, and as the soldiers watched the torrent of water, they appreciated the wisdom of the prophet who commanded them to dig ditches.

After great storms, the beds of rivers quickly fill until the currents become impassable. Yet when the storm abates and the rain ceases, the stream quickly disappears. If the soldiers had not prepared ditches, the river would have subsided, and the need of the armies would have remained unchanged. Elisha's foresight was remarkable, for after the torrent had passed, sufficient water remained in the ditches to quench the thirst of that expeditionary force. God sees the end from the beginning, and happy are the people who follow His directions.

The Provision of God . . . *How Abundant*

"That valley shall be filled with water, that ye may drink, both ye, and your cattle, and your beasts. And this is but a light thing in the sight of the LORD: he will deliver the Moabites also into your hand . . . and the country was filled with water" (2 Kings 3:17–20).

It should be remembered that to feed three armies it was necessary to have many animals available for slaughter. Dromedaries can carry sufficient water over great distances, but cattle need water every day. God was very generous! He saw the immense need of the men and beasts and sent sufficient supplies for their survival.

To curb the aggression of Iraq against Kuwait, a multi-national force went to Saudi Arabia, and vast supplies of material were necessary to sustain hundreds of thousands of men. It was interesting to hear American soldiers saying by means of radio and television, "Send us water!" Special ships were sent carrying this invaluable commodity. To understand this problem is to appreciate the desperation with which the ancient kings sought the assistance of Elisha. They recognized the fact that without help they would die in that merciless desert. Sometimes the Lord permits His people to get into trouble so that their understanding may be increased. Only then are they able to exclaim, "God is our refuge and strength, a very present help in trouble" (Ps. 46:1). The stillness that filled the camp during the offering of the meat offering was suddenly shattered as exultant soldiers rushed toward the ditches to plunge their faces into the refreshing water. Nevertheless, that was only a part of the deliverance which God had promised. He had said, "And this is but a light thing in the sight of the LORD."

The Power of God . . . *How Amazing*

"And when all the Moabites heard that the kings were come up to fight against them, they gathered all that were able to put on armor and upward, and stood in the border. And they rose up early in the morning, and the sun shone upon the water, and the Moabites saw the water on the other side as red as blood: And they said, This is blood: the kings are surely slain, and they have smitten one another: now therefore, Moab, to the spoil. And when they came to the camp of Israel, the Israelites rose up and smote the Moabites, so that they fled before them: but they went forward smiting the Moabites, even in their country" (2 Kings 3:21–24).

The Rev. G. Rawlinson, writing in *The Pulpit Commentary*, says, "The Wady-el Haday drains a portion of Southern Moab and also a considerable tract of Northern Edom. The nocturnal storm had burst, not in the Moabite country where it would have attracted the attention of the Moabites, but in some comparatively distant part of the Idumaean territory . . . The red hue of the water is ascribed by Ewald to the red tinge of the soil in the part of Edom where the rain had fallen . . . and by Keil to 'the reddish earth of the freshly dug trenches," but the only cause of the redness mentioned in Kings or Josephus is the ruddy hue of the sunrise. The red light falling upon the water in the pits and reflecting the opposite side of the Wady would account for the mistake of the Moabites who concluded the red-looking liquid was blood" (*The Pulpit Commentary*, 2 Kings, pp. 45–46).

Believing their enemies had embarked upon a course of self-destruction, the Moabites attacked the camp of the Israelites only to discover their assumption was wrong. The three armies were waiting for the assault, and in the ensuing battle the attackers were slain or put to flight.

Each detail of the ancient account supplies evidence that God can do the impossible. The sending of the storm, the time of the arrival of the water, the effect of whatever it was that made the river appear as blood, the mistaken assumption of the Moabites, and the ultimate triumph of God's people suggest that throughout the entire episode everything was controlled by the Almighty. Outstanding among the many onlookers was Elisha, who knew God would do what He promised. When Jehovah divided the Red Sea, "the waters were a wall unto them on their right hand, and on their left" (Ex. 14:22). Yet, when He sent floods rushing down the ancient wadi, the people were commanded to dig ditches which would retain the precious water. These verses suggest that God is equal to every emergency in life, but He expects obedient cooperation from His people. He does not do everything!

During my stay in South Africa I spoke at a Bible Conference in the district known as the Karroo where the land is irrigated. Every rancher is expected to prepare for the time when water is released from a dam in the distant mountains. Ditches have to be free of obstruction, and the soil graded to enable the water to reach all parts of the farms. I shall always remember a man who testified in one of the meetings. He said, "You all know me. I did not wish to come to these meetings, but I came anyhow! Do you know what I have been doing? I took a shovel and have been opening the channels in my soul. Thank God the water is flowing again. My ditches were all clogged up!" The prophet Ezekiel was correct when he said, "And every thing shall live whither the river cometh" (Ezek. 47:9). It would seem also that David had endured through a similar experience for he wrote, "Weeping may endure for a night, but joy cometh in the morning" (Ps. 30:5). All people should know that rivers of living water will surely come, if they remain close to the Lamb of God and the place where He was sacrificed.

> Jesus keep me near the cross;
> There a precious fountain,
> Free to all, a healing stream
> Flows from Calvary's mountain.
>
> F. J. Crosby

During my ministry in Canada I enjoyed the privilege of working with a very fine minister who was also the chaplain at the local prison. He told me of a sad experience when he walked with a prisoner to the place of execution. The convicted criminal came from the far north of Canada where he had been an official guide. Unfortunately, he had come to work in one of the southern cities and had associated with people who led him into a life of crime. One night in a drunken rage, he murdered a man and ultimately was sentenced to death. My friend asked if he had ever heard about Jesus and was astonished to hear his reply. "Yes, I heard about Him once. A missionary visiting the north country asked if I knew Jesus. I thought for a while and then replied, 'No! There is nobody homesteading in these parts with that name.'"

After several visits the convicted man accepted Christ as his Savior, and the change in his outlook was amazing. It was impossible to question his sincerity, but the law was unrelenting. As the chaplain accompanied him to the scaffold, he read from Psalm 23, "Yea, though I walk through the valley of the shadow of death, I will fear no evil: for thou art with me; thy rod and thy staff they comfort me." My friend was extremely sad when he described how the prisoner said, *"If only I had heard about Him earlier."* Christians know the Savior and should testify concerning His power to save. Their failure to do so might lead to tragedy.

Naaman . . . *The Diplomatic Captain* (2 Kings 5:18)

The Syrian captain was probably a man with a commanding personality. Admired by his king and respected by his soldiers, he had gained considerable notoriety. His triumphs in battle had won an immortal place in the history of his nation. It is depressing to read, "Now Naaman, captain of the host of the king of Syria, was a great man with his master, and honorable, because by him the LORD had given deliverance unto Syria: he was also a mighty man in valor, *but he was a leper*" (2 Kings 5:1). It is not known when the illustrious warrior first became a leper, but the news of the tragedy spread quickly through the land, and every citizen was filled with intense pity for the man whose exploits had made him famous.

Naaman had been sent to the king of Israel and after varying interludes had reached the home of the prophet Elisha, by whom he was instructed to bathe seven times in the river Jordan. His intense disappointment and anger had been apparent when he said, "Are not Abana and Pharpar, rivers of Damascus, better than all the waters of Israel? may I not wash in them, and be clean?" (2 Kings 5:12). His reluctance to obey the prophet's command was overcome by the intercession of his servants, and the miracle which followed is now known throughout the world.

The captain was humbled when he returned to the servant of God but was amazed when Elisha refused payment for his services. He had never known a Syrian priest to refuse remuneration for anything! The prophet was very accommodating when the soldier sought permission to take some of Israel's soil back to Syria. His intention to build an earthen altar seemed to indicate the immensity of the gratitude filling his soul. The determination to remain true to the God of his salvation appeared to be obvious when he said, "Thy servant will henceforth offer neither burnt offering nor sacrifice unto other gods, but unto the LORD" (2 Kings 5:17). Then the captain hesitated; he was not sure how his final request would be received. Trouble awaited him in his homeland. Fellow countrymen would organize a huge celebration for his return, and a time of national thanksgiving would be proclaimed throughout Syria. The temple of Rimmon would be filled to capacity by enthusiastic worshipers, and even the king would prostrate himself in humble gratitude before the idol. When Naaman frowned, the prophet surely asked the cause of his discomfort. The Syrian explained, saying, "In this thing the Lord pardon thy servant, that when my master goeth into the house of Rimmon to worship there, and he leaneth on my hand . . . *when I bow down myself in the house of Rimmon,* the LORD pardon thy servant in this thing" (2 Kings 5:18). Probably Elisha was disappointed when he replied, "Go in peace," for he knew Naaman was about to lose his greatest opportunity.

The famous temple was packed with eager worshipers. The priests were standing before the towering image of Rimmon, and everyone eagerly awaited the arrival of the king and his illustrious servant. When the bugles sounded, the ornate doors of the pagan sanctuary opened, and the audience smiled as they saw their ruler leaning on the arm of the man whose deliverance they had come to celebrate. The service of thanksgiving commenced, and the high priest reminded the people of the immense debt owed to the idol whose presence dominated the assembly. The king's face was radiant, but apprehension seemed to interfere with the happiness of the famous captain. He dreaded the moment when everyone would be expected to bow before the god who was being praised for something he had not accomplished. Perhaps even angels were hushed when in conformity with the usual procedure, Naaman bowed before the idol. He was publicly acknowledging his debt to a god he had professed to abandon. The poor man had contracted lockjaw! He could have been the greatest evangelist ever heard in Syria, but alas, he was silenced by fear. Was he afraid of losing favor with the royal household and scared he might lose his popularity? The answer to those questions may never be known, but it is undeniable that many thousands of pagans might have been introduced to the God of Israel.

Nicodemus . . . *The Distinguished Counselor* (John 7:50–53)

The Jewish Council Chamber was hushed; a distinguished leader was about to address the assembly. Every person present listened intently, for Nicodemus was a brilliant orator. He would know how to solve the problem which threatened the country. The recurring arguments concerning Jesus of Nazareth were frustrating and tiresome; the situation demanded immediate action. The Speaker of the House used his gavel and invited the eminent ruler to take the floor.

"Nicodemus saith unto them, (he that came to Jesus by night, being one of them,) Doth our law judge any man before it hear him, and know what he doeth? They answered and said unto him, Art thou also of Galilee? Search, and look: for out of Galilee ariseth no prophet. And every man went unto his own house." Crestfallen and ashamed, Nicodemus joined his colleagues as they went into the streets of Jerusalem. He had lost the opportunity of a lifetime and could never outlive his remorse. Even Jesus had recognized his stature within the nation, for He had identified him as *the* teacher of the nation (see John 3:10, *The Amplified Bible*). The ruler had earlier sought an interview with the Savior because he desired information as to whether or not Jesus was the expected Messiah (see the author's *John's Wonderful Gospel*, Kregel Publications, 1962, p. 78). The eminent theologian would have known that Daniel predicted the arrival of the Messiah, and had even described His death. Furthermore, the time mentioned had expired thirty years earlier, and since there was not another prophet to be compared with Jesus of Nazareth, the knowledge and oratorical ability of the greatest teacher in Israel could have made tremendous impressions within that assembly. That he was silenced by a rude statement in the chamber remains one of the greatest tragedies of the New Testament. The counselor might have covered himself with honor had he not suffered from an acute case of lockjaw.

Nicodemus probably thought he was the only believer in the assembly, but he was mistaken; there was another man, Joseph of Arimathea, who listened intently as Nicodemus made his brief statement. The speaker abruptly terminated his speech, and his colleague concluded *he* was the only disciple in the Sanhedrin.

When Nicodemus sat quietly in the Sanhedrin chamber, he remembered the occasion when he had been enthralled in the presence of Jesus. He probably believed that if Christ could be invited to address the House, other members would also admire the wonderful Man from Nazareth. It is impossible to know what tremendous effects might have followed if he had not been hushed by the aggressive attitude of his critics. It would have made exciting reading if John could have described how the great ruler of the Jews had transformed a parliamentary session into an evangelistic service. Unfortunately, his talent was left buried in the sands of silence, and although later he went with Joseph to lay the body of Jesus to rest, he could never erase from his memory the fact that when Christ needed a friend, he had remained silent.

Gamaliel . . . *The Discreet Coward* (Acts 5:34–40)

He was a polished advocate, an eminent and internationally famous scholar. Gamaliel was the president of the Hebrew theological seminary, and possibly the greatest intellectual authority within the nation. When he spoke, men listened. Outside the government building Jerusalem was in an uproar. The streets were crowded with excited people, and according to popular report, obstinate fishermen from Galilee were the cause of the trouble. The men had miraculously escaped from prison and were again disturbing the peace. The agitators had been apprehended and escorted to the Senate building. Their attitude and remarks were extremely uncompromising, and the angry rulers hardly knew how to handle the situation. Most of the counselors favored the death penalty for the upstart rebels, but a final decision had been made.

"Then stood there up one in the council, a Pharisee named Gamaliel, a doctor of the law, had in reputation among all the people, and commanded to put the apostles forth a little space." The extent of the man's influence may be measured by his ability to command. His words were authoritative, and the accused men were removed to an adjacent chamber. The speech then delivered by the eminent educator was expressed with dignity and eloquence hard to resist. After presenting his irrefutable argument, Gamaliel said, "Refrain from these men, and let them alone: for if this counsel or this work be of men, it will come to nought: But if it be of God, ye cannot overthrow it; lest haply ye be found to fight against God." His speech was unanimously approved. "And when they had called the apostles, and beaten them, they commanded that they should not speak in the name of Jesus, and let them go."

Dr. Gamaliel returned to his home, but it is doubtful that he slept that night. He had delivered a convincing speech and saved the lives of the accused men. Nevertheless he had not protested when the prisoners were flogged. According to his own deductions, future events would decide his course of action. The new movement called Christianity would either diminish or conquer the world. The theologian might be forced to make difficult decisions which might destroy his popularity throughout the nation.

The impossible had taken place, but it was difficult to believe that one of the graduates from the Hebrew college had become a Christian. Saul of Tarsus, who had been commissioned by the High Priest to destroy heretics, had undergone a startling experience. It was said he had met the risen Christ and embraced the alien faith. The people were filled with excitement and wondered what would happen next. Gamaliel had warned about the possibility of fighting against Jehovah and had assured his colleagues that if the new doctrines were contrary to the will of God, the movement would perish. Probably many people asked what the scholar would do if the condemned movement continued to increase. As time passed, Gamaliel heard more and more about the exploits of his former student. Roman soldiers were being won for Christ, and along the highways of Europe and Asia preachers were making known the gospel which Paul had earlier condemned.

Gamaliel had been a true prophet; his words had been fulfilled, and it was becoming evident that men could not fight against God and win. The theologian considered his future actions. If he followed Jesus of Nazareth, he would lose his position as Chancellor of the University, be deprived of his income, and many would consider him a traitor to the ancient faith. Perhaps he should wait a little longer. He did and eventually disappeared into obscurity. He might have been one of Paul's greatest helpers, but unfortunately he developed lockjaw and that problem ruined his future and possibly destroyed his soul.

The Prisoners in Babylon . . . *The Despondent Captives* (Psalm 137:1–3)

There were many captives in Babylon, but not all were idolaters. During the long hot days the slaves were forced to make bricks and erect walls, and the merciless lashes of whips made their tasks intolerable. When the shadows of evening lengthened, the laborers were permitted to cool their feet in the river and lean against hovels to remember their homeland. Those Hebrews had learned life's most important lessons in a school of suffering. It had been a bitter experience. Even the twinkling stars seemed to mock them. One of the captives supplied a word-picture of those horrendous evenings. He wrote, "By the rivers of Babylon, there we sat down, yea, we wept, when we remembered Zion. We hanged our harps upon the willows in the midst thereof. For there they that carried us away captive required of us a song; and they that wasted us required of us mirth, saying, Sing us one of the songs of Zion. How shall we sing the Lord's song in a strange land? If I forget thee, O Jerusalem, let my right hand forget her cunning. If I do not remember thee, let my tongue cleave to the roof of my mouth; if I prefer not Jerusalem above my chief joy."

The Babylonians did not understand the captives were unable to sing when their hearts were broken. Mirth was never the child of sorrow. Those suffering people could not produce symphonies when the strings of their souls refused to vibrate. Praise never fills lives when memories are painful. People who once served the Lord and whose folly led them into bondage can only be filled with remorse. The poet was correct when he wrote:

> The peaceful hours I once enjoyed;
> How sweet the memory still:
> But they have left an aching void,
> The world can never fill.

There is no night as dark as that in which the Light of the World never shines. It was written of Judas that "he went out and it was night." Did that unfortunate man reminisce before he placed the rope around his neck and remember the occasions when he walked with the Savior? Did he sigh when he remembered going through the highways and byways of Palestine proclaiming the glorious news of salvation? Poor man, he had much in common with the Babylonian captives; it was difficult to sing praises when his soul was filled with haunting accusations. He would never again sing the melodies of heaven, for he had lost his music in a sea of guilt. Unfortunately many people are still making the same mistake. They forget that people who play with fire eventually become burned.

MANASSEH, THE SON WHO BROKE
HIS MOTHER'S HEART

"Manasseh was twelve years old when he began to reign, and reigned fifty and five years in Jerusalem. And his mother's name was Hephzibah. And he did that which was evil in the sight of the Lord" (2 Kings 21:1–2).

It has often been claimed that behind every successful man stands a dedicated woman. Paul was probably the greatest evangelist ever to serve the church, but he might not have known the Savior had not his devoted sister prayed him into the kingdom of Christ. When he was a student in the seminary of Gamaliel, Paul stayed with that woman who ultimately became a Christian. Her grief must have been enormous when her brother began persecuting the followers of the Savior. Later when the apostle wrote to the church in Rome, he mentioned her and said she "was in Christ before me" (Rom. 16:7).

Manasseh was the Old Testament equivalent of Saul of Tarsus. He was the son of Hezekiah and Hephzibah, the king and queen of Judah but, unlike them, was a terrible person who slaughtered God's people and filled Jerusalem with the blood of innocent people. Yet before he died, this abominable man repented of his sin and returned to the God of his parents. His mother's name was Hephzibah, which means "My delight is in her." When she was born her mother's eyes possibly shone with delight, and the baby was given an illustrious name. The parents sincerely believed that God had special pleasure in the child who eventually became the queen of Israel. It is significant that she became the wife of Hezekiah, the royal reformer who spread out a threatening letter before the Lord so that Jehovah could read for Himself what the insulting king of Babylon had said. There can be no doubt that Queen Hephzibah helped her husband in all the major decisions which were made; her influence was known throughout the nation. When her child was born, she had great hopes for the future, but unfortunately, her heart filled with pain when she saw him destroying everything of value within the kingdom. She could do little but pray, and it is possible the happy ending to the tragic history of Manasseh was the result of her continuing intercession.

Rejecting an Old Faith . . . *Rebellion*

This is the account of a teenage boy who believed he knew everything! He was self-assured, and the opinion of his parents meant nothing. Manasseh decided to please himself in everything he did. The young upstart destroyed all the good accomplished by his deceased father and installed his own idol within the tabernacle. He violated the commands of God and turned the Holy City into a cesspool of iniquity. The man was like the prodigal son who despised his home, rejected his father's love, and departed to live a shameful life. It is difficult to explain why some of the most devoted parents have rebellious children.

When God addressed His decadent nation, He said, "For my people have committed two evils; they have forsaken me the fountain of living waters, and hewed them out cisterns, broken cisterns, that can hold no water" (Jer. 2:13). Those words could have been spoken to the wayward son of Hezekiah. Manasseh completely rejected the teaching and example of his parents and forsook the source of all spiritual refreshment. A fountain of living water was an invaluable asset in a land where water was hard to find. It quenched the thirst of travelers and maintained the life of people, who, without it, would have died. The words of the Savior have been fulfilled in all ages, "If any man thirst, let him come unto me and drink" (John 7:37).

When a man is deprived of living water, he searches elsewhere to find what his soul needs, but the substitute can never equal the original. The cisterns created by man develop cracks and hold no water. The prophet, Haggai, expressed this fact when he said, "Ye have sown much, and bring in little; ye eat, but ye have not enough; ye drink, but ye are not filled with drink; ye clothe you, but there is none warm; and he that earneth wages earneth wages to put it into *a bag with holes*" (Hag. 1:6). The poet wrote:

> I tried the broken cisterns, Lord,
> But, ah, the waters failed;
> E'en as I stopped to drink, they fled,
> And mocked me as I wailed.

Manasseh, the king of Judah, had a great deal to learn, but like many other people, he learned the hard way!

Repeating an Old Folly . . . *Ruinous*

"And he caused his children to pass through the fire in the valley of the son of Hinnom: also he observed times, and used enchantments, and used witchcraft, and dealt with a familiar spirit, and with wizards: he wrought much evil in the sight of the Lord, to provoke him to anger. And he set a carved image, the idol which he had made, in the house of God" (2 Chron. 33:6–7). The man was driven by an irrepressible urge; he was at war with himself. Each act of defiance was followed by a greater atrocity. He began by emulating the example supplied by adjacent nations; he made his children the victims of fiery sacrifices. Then he associated with wizards and endeavored to commune with the dead—perhaps his own children. These deeds were forbidden by God, but the arrogant king did what he desired. He was on a course of self-destruction, the end of which was never in doubt. His cisterns began to crack, and finally he was destitute.

"And the LORD spake to Manasseh, and to his people: but they would not hearken. Wherefore the LORD brought upon them the captains of the host of the king of Assyria, which took Manasseh among the thorns, and bound him with fetters, and carried him to Babylon" (2 Chron. 33:10–11). The statement that says Manasseh was taken among the thorns is interesting. The same word is translated in 2 Kings 19:28 as hook, "Therefore I will put my hook in thy nose." The captive was bound with chains of brass and pulled by a hook inserted into the nose. This indignity reduced the king to the level of a common slave. The prayers of his godly parents were answered even though they had died. "God moves in a mysterious way His wonders to perform," says the poet Cowper. Sometimes, the Lord has to punish a man to restore his sanity. It is better to hurt a person than to lose him forever. If Manasseh were taken among the thorns, it would be a perfect indication of the folly of forsaking the Lord. With all his wealth and popularity, the best resting place available was a bed of thorns! It would be impossible to sleep peacefully with pointed reminders of his irreligious stupidity.

Relying on an Old Fact . . . *Repentance*

"And when he was in affliction, he besought the Lord his God, and humbled himself greatly before the God of his fathers, And prayed unto him: and he was entreated of him, and heard his supplication, and brought him again to Jerusalem into his kingdom. Then Manasseh knew that the LORD he was God" (2 Chron. 33:12–13). This is one of the brightest stars shining in the darkness of Israel's history. During an age when Jehovah was feared more than loved, it was astonishing to discover this revelation of the matchless grace of God. Manasseh, whose sinful deeds were unequalled by any contemporary, would have appreciated the words of John Wesley:

> Depth of Mercy! can there be
> Mercy still reserved for me?
> Can my God His wrath forbear
> Me—the chief of sinners spare?
>
> I have long withstood His grace,
> Long provoked Him to His face,
> Would not hearken to His calls,
> Grieved Him by a thousand falls.
>
> If I rightly read Thy heart,
> If Thou all compassion art,
> Bow Thine ear, in mercy bow,
> Pardon and accept me now.

This section of the story may best be considered under three headings: God was wise, willing, and wonderful.

(1) *God was Wise.* Solomon said, "The Lord by wisdom hath founded the earth; by understanding hath he established the heavens" (Prov. 3:19). Many other things were brought into being by the omniscience of the Almighty. Queen Hephzibah might have asked many things for her stubborn child, but it is extremely doubtful whether she would have asked that he be humiliated and taken to an alien land. Sometimes it is difficult to understand the actions of God, but He is too wise to make a mistake and too loving to be unkind. Occasionally, the Lord chastens rebellious people, but the hand that holds the rod is always called love. Jehovah permitted Manasseh to become a captive because more could be done for his soul in Babylon than could be accomplished in Jerusalem.

(2) *God was Willing.* "And God heard his supplication and brought him again to Jerusalem into his kingdom." It is not known how this was done, for few monarchs were ever restored to their kingdom by enemies. The Lord not only heard the prayer of the repentant sinner, He influenced the king of Babylon to show kindness to his infamous prisoner. That this mercy was entirely undeserved was apparent, but "where sin abounded, grace did much more abound" (Rom. 5:20).

(3) *God was Wonderful.* It appeared to be incomprehensible that the Lord should be merciful when Manasseh had done so much to desecrate His name. It had always been taught that a sinner reaped what he sowed, and the terrible deeds of this king deserved retribution of the greatest kind. Paul, who never forgot his past, would have understood why the grace of God was extended to Manasseh. The Lord always delighted in kindness, but what then was only a glimpse of the divine attribute was destined to become an enthralling vision. It is refreshing to know that from everlasting to everlasting, Jehovah remains changeless. "For as the heaven is high above the earth, so great is his mercy toward them that fear him" (Ps. 103:11).

Rejoicing in an Old Fellowship . . . *Responsibility*

"Now the rest of the acts of Manasseh, and his prayer unto his God, and the words of the seers that spake to him in the name of the LORD God of Israel, behold, they are written in the book of the kings of Israel" (2 Chron. 33:18). It is significant that when Manasseh began his new life, he endeavored to remove the evil things that had been introduced when he was defiant and arrogant. The historian describes how he removed the idol that had been installed in the house of God, and throughout the nation, people were encouraged to worship Jehovah. Conversion without contrition leaves much to be desired. Even Zacchaeus understood that necessity when he said, "Behold, Lord, the half of my goods I give to the poor; and if I have taken anything from any man by false accusation, I restore him fourfold" (Luke 19:8).

Manasseh restored what had been lost, and that should be an example all Christians should emulate. To love God means to please Him. So many people rejoice in His forgiveness but forget they might owe much to people who were previously hurt. To avoid offending the tax gatherers, Christ sent Peter to catch a fish, find a coin in its mouth, and use the money to pay the taxes. Christians should be willing to do anything to destroy an evil influence which still lingers in the minds of former associates. The reference to "*the seers*" who spoke to Manasseh stimulates thought. Did they speak words of warning during his unregenerate days or encouragement after his return from Babylon? Perhaps they ministered on both occasions, and when the king submitted himself to God, the advice of the prophets became invaluable. Under their direction, idols were destroyed, and the altar of God was restored to its proper place in the tabernacle. The monarch valued the company of men previously ignored. The transformation within his heart and country beggared description. It is not known if the saints in heaven are permitted to see the people remaining on earth, but if they are, it would be safe to conclude that Hephzibah, the mother of Manasseh, looked upon her boy and smiled. Her prayers had been answered.

"I will lift up mine eyes unto the hills,
from whence cometh my help" (Ps. 121:1).

It is interesting to note that although the arrangement of the Psalms may not be chronologically correct, Psalm 121 is the perfect continuation of Psalm 120. Evidently the organizer was supervised by the Holy Spirit. Between the two sonnets there is a journey from the depths of depression to heights of ecstasy, from the oppressive limitations of a dense fog to the clear vision of magnificent expectation. Within the framework of Psalm 120, the writer mentioned distress, lying lips, deceitful tongues, sharp arrows, burning coals, hateful people, and warmongers. His soul was overwhelmed with problems, his outlook bleak, and his future threatened. Then suddenly things changed. As a thrilling hope filled his soul, David said, "I will lift up mine eyes unto the hills from whence cometh my help." A great resolve had gripped him, and he was determined to focus his vision upon the Lord who had been his refuge in trouble. He referred to God as his *Keeper*, *Watchman*, and the *Guardian* of his soul. Perhaps he was thinking about the city employees whose trained eyes watched for the approach of enemies. They were reliable men, implicitly trusted by the people. Their dedication to duty guaranteed the safety of the citizens. David compared that situation with his own soul where the Lord was a constant sentinel. The fear expressed in Psalm 120 was replaced by fellowship, and the lies of David's enemies were forgotten as he remembered the promises of God. The renewal of the king's trust in Jehovah revived his impoverished soul. Psalm 121 is one of the most reassuring of all David's sonnets.

How Safe . . . *"The Lord is thy keeper"* (Psalm 121:5)

Certain qualifications were necessary for all men who aspired to be the watchmen of any city; they were required to be vigilant, trustworthy, and courageous. If the men did not exhibit such attributes, they were not accepted by the elders. The cities were surrounded by high walls, and when danger threatened, everyone retired within their stronghold. When an alarm was heard, people prepared to defend their property. Any official who slept when on duty was considered unworthy of trust. The same facts applied to those who guarded the vineyards. Each parcel of land had its watchtower where men resided to safeguard the vines. Wild pigs were a menace and could destroy property overnight.

It was not a cause for amazement when David compared his soul with the vineyards. He was encouraged by the fact that Jehovah was his Keeper. God's ability was sufficient to protect everybody. David realized the Guardian of his vineyard was also the Good Shepherd, within whose fold he was perfectly safe.

How Sheltered . . . *"The Lord is thy shade upon thy right hand"*
(Psalm 121:5)

Throughout the vast expanse of Eastern deserts, shade was hard to locate. The limitless horizons of sandy wilderness often became a nightmare for desperate travelers. The sun shone mercilessly upon a barren landscape, and fresh water was impossible to find. Occasionally stony outcrops could be reached, and during devastating sandstorms these provided limited protection against nature's onslaught. Travelers accustomed to desert conditions knew where such shade could be found and hurriedly sought shelter when sandstorms were approaching.

David wrote in Psalm 91:1, "He that dwelleth in the secret place of the most High shall abide under the shadow of the Almighty." He compared *the shady place* with *the secret place*—within both the soul could find refuge. The shade from excessive heat and glare offered temporary relief; *abiding* in the secret place of the most High expressed a blessedness which could last forever.

> There is a place of quiet rest,
> Near to the heart of God,
> A place where sin cannot molest,
> Near to the heart of God.
>
> O Jesus blest Redeemer,
> Sent from the heart of God,
> Hold us who wait before Thee,
> Near to the heart of God.
> Cleland B. McAfee, 1866–1944.

How Secure . . . *"The Lord shall preserve thee from all evil"*
(Psalm 121:7)

Safety suggests protection; shelter offers peace; security promises prosperity. Whether the Christian goes out to battle or home to rest, the presence of God guarantees success. It was easy for the children of Israel to believe this fact, for the cloud above the tabernacle by day and the pillar of fire by night signified Jehovah was always with His people. He was a shield between them and the enemy. That explained their military success.

When the Hebrews left Egypt they had no military experience nor weapons; the people were a disorganized multitude. Moses received some training in the Egyptian Army, but without the help of Jehovah the nation would have perished in the wilderness. That the Lord promised protection from *all evil* revealed the magnitude of His capability. The significant superiority of other nations became meaningless when God displayed His irresistible might. Often when Israel was about to be overwhelmed, the prophet of God stood majestically before the enemy and seemed to hold the future in his hand. "And when the servant of the man of God was risen early, and gone forth, behold an host compassed the city both with horses and chariots. And his servant said unto him, Alas, my master! how shall we do? And he answered, Fear not; for they that be with us are more than they that be with them. And Elisha prayed, and said, LORD, I pray thee, open his eyes, that he may see. And the LORD opened the eyes of the young man; and he saw; and behold, the mountain was full of horses and chariots of fire round about Elisha. And when they came down to him, Elisha prayed unto the LORD, and said, Smite this people, I pray thee, with blindness. And he smote them with blindness according to the word of Elisha" (2 Kings 6:15–18).

It is worthy of consideration that God's protecting forces were present even before the young man's eyes were opened. Their presence guaranteed the safety of God's believing servant.

How Special . . . *"The sun shall not smite thee by day, nor the moon by night"* (Psalm 121:6)

The Psalmist said, "Ye that love the LORD, hate evil; he preserveth the souls of his saints; he delivereth them out of the hand of the wicked" (Ps. 97:10). The ancient songwriter evidently believed divine protection was conditional. God did not preserve all people irrespective of their spirituality. The injunction to "hate evil" placed a moral obligation upon all who desired His assistance. The grace of God could be seen by all people, but His glory was shared only with saints. The psalmist emphasized that God "preserveth the souls of his saints." The Savior expressed similar truth when He said, "Are not two sparrows sold for a farthing? and one of them shall not fall on the ground without your Father. But the very hairs of your head are all numbered. Fear ye not therefore, ye are of more value than many sparrows" (Matt. 10:29–31).

After a prairie fire in Australia a farmer went to survey the damage done to his property. As he walked through a yard, he disturbed a charred mass on the ground and was astonished when a family of small chicks emerged from the burnt feathers. He realized that a hen had given her life for her family and was reminded of that greater sacrifice when Christ died for those He loved. Moses was correct when in addressing Israel he said, "For thou art an holy people unto the LORD thy God: The LORD thy God hath chosen thee to be a special people unto himself, above all people that are upon the face of the earth" (Deut. 7:6). That Israel occupied such a place in the affections of the Almighty indicated His continued watchfulness over them. That kind of love deserved to be reciprocated.

How Splendid . . . *"The Lord shall preserve thy going out and thy coming in, from this time forth, and even for evermore"* (Psalm 121:8)

David knew that some professions of friendship failed to stand the test of time; they seldom endured through continuing hardship. Even members of the royal family had been rebellious. Absalom had been guilty of insurrection, yet other people had remained loyal to the king even amid the most distressing episodes of his life (see 2 Sam. 17:27–29). True friends were more desirable than gold. Yet David realized that even his most loyal comrades could not be compared with the Lord. Human assistance could only continue until death, but the favor of the Lord was for "evermore." It lasted through time and into eternity. When David reminisced, it was easy to remember occasions when God enabled him to overcome very difficult circumstances. The triumph over Goliath was only one example of how strength had been made perfect in David's weakness. Oftentimes when death appeared to be imminent, the king relied upon the unfailing promises of God and exclaimed: "Yea, though I walk through the valley of the shadow of death, I will fear no evil: for thou art with me; thy rod and thy staff they comfort me" (Ps. 23:4). David looked back with gratitude and onward with confidence; his heavenly Father was reliable.

"And let the king appoint officers in all the provinces of his kingdom, that they may gather together all the fair young virgins unto Shushan the palace, to the house of the women, unto the custody of Hege the king's chamberlain, keeper of the women; and let their things for purification be given them. And let the maiden which pleaseth the king be queen instead of Vashti. And the thing pleased the king; and he did so" (Esther 2:3–4).

The book of Esther has become famous for two reasons. Although the record is included in the canon of Holy Scripture, God was never mentioned by Mordecai, the author. Reasons for the omission are debatable, for there were many occasions when the writer could easily have referred to the Almighty. Throughout the history of the Hebrew nation God's protecting hand was never more evident than in the deliverance wrought through the ingenuity and courage of a Hebrew girl.

Secondly, the book is unique in that, as far as is known, it describes the first beauty pageant in history. The modern world has become accustomed to occasions when young ladies from many nations compete for the honor of becoming Miss Universe, and the amazing spectacle is televised around the world. The drama and excitement deepen when, by a process of elimination, the competitors decrease in number until only a few stand before the international audience. Ultimately the winner is named, and the new queen is crowned. Every year the spectacle is watched by millions of people who do not know the first and greatest pageant was arranged in Susa or Shushan, the ancient capital of the Elamite empire which was situated in the country now called Iran. The winner of that contest was destined to reign—not for twelve months, but for the rest of her life over an empire which reached ". . . from India even unto Ethiopia, over an hundred and seven and twenty provinces" (Esther 1:1). The girl who won that beauty competition could not have known that her name was to become famous throughout the world. She was destined to become the instrument of Jehovah, the unseen God, who planned and directed her every movement.

The Royal Refusal . . . *Unprecedented*

"The king made a feast unto all the people that were present in Shushan the palace, both unto great and small, seven days, in the court of the garden of the king's palace; Where were white, green and blue hangings, fastened with cords of fine linen and purple to silver rings and pillars of marble: the beds were of gold and silver, upon a pavement of red, and blue, and white, and black marble. And they gave them drink in vessels of gold (the vessels being diverse one from another), and royal wine in abundance . . . On the seventh day, when the heart of the king was merry with wine, he commanded . . . To bring Vashti the queen before the king with the crown royal, to shew the people and the princes her beauty: for she was fair to look on . . . But the queen Vashti refused to come" (Esther 1:5–12).

The queen's refusal to obey her husband's command was unprecedented; it was suicidal! Even men hastened to grant the king's requests, but for a woman to insult her royal master was unpardonable. She shamed him before an international assembly of very important guests. Why she was rebellious was never revealed. Perhaps she knew her husband was drunk and refused to be made a spectacle at the royal party. On the other hand, since she had convened her own banquet, she may have disliked the idea of ruining her plans to please a selfish husband. Nevertheless, it was unthinkable to offend the king in whose hand was the power of life and death. No woman for any reason would have acted as she did. Therefore, the conclusion is inescapable; she was influenced by an irresistible force which came from God.

The Remarkable Reception . . . *Unexpected*

"Now in Shushan the palace there was a certain Jew, whose name was Mordecai . . . Who had been carried away from Jerusalem . . . whom Nebuchadnezzar the king of Babylon had carried away. And he brought up Hadassah, that is, Esther, his uncle's daughter: for she had neither father nor mother, and the maid was fair and beautiful; whom Mordecai, when her father and mother were dead, took for his own daughter" (Esther 2:5–7). When all the consternation at the royal banquet had subsided, plans were made to choose a new queen and search was made throughout the land for the most attractive maidens. To that first beauty pageant the adopted daughter of Mordecai was brought, and her indescribable charm captivated everybody. Even the keeper of the women was impressed. "And the maiden pleased him, and she obtained kindness of him" (Esther 2:9). Actually, there was no contest. The competition was over before it commenced. That was phenomenal, for Esther was a Jewish slave. Beauty is a great asset, but it seldom overcomes prejudice. What influenced the mind of the official and paved the way for an orphan to become queen of a vast empire? The sun shines even when clouds fill the sky!

The Reported Rebellion . . . *Unrewarded*

"In those days, while Mordecai sat in the king's gate, two of the king's chamberlains . . . sought to lay hand on the king Ahasuerus. And the thing was known to Mordecai, who told it unto Esther the queen; and Esther certified the king thereof in Mordecai's name. And when inquisition was made of the matter, it was found out; therefore they were both hanged on a tree; and it was written in the book of the chronicles before the king" (Esther 2:21–23).

It is difficult to understand how any monarch should remain ungrateful to a man who had just prevented his assassination. It is hard to believe that Esther the queen did not suggest a reward for her uncle. Neither did Mordecai complain of the royal indifference. At a later date he was not reluctant to express his opinions, and Esther was active in making her husband acknowledge his responsibility. How could such an important event be ignored or forgotten—unless God was directing the proceedings!

The Remembered Record . . . *Unusual*

The subsequent villany of Haman, who detested all Jews, is known throughout the world. Both Mordecai and his adopted daughter must have wondered why God, who had done so much to help them, now seemed to have forgotten His people. During the night before what might have become the most tragic day in Hebrew history, the king could not sleep, "and he commanded to bring the book of records of the chronicles; and they were read before the king. And it was found written, that Mordecai had told of Bigthana and Teresh, two of the king's chamberlains . . . who sought to lay hands on the king Ahasuerus. And the king said, What honor and dignity hath been done to Mordecai for this? Then said the king's servants that ministered unto him, There is nothing done for him" (Esther 6:1–3). The marginal reading suggests that "the king's sleep fled away," and curious readers wonder how this was accomplished.

Even if the poor man possessed all the sleeping pills in the world, sleep would have been impossible, for God was determined to keep him awake. It seems extraordinary that, in the middle of the night, the frustrated monarch should seek consolation from his archives! How could historical records produce slumber? Probably there were many entries in those scrolls, but in some strange way the unknown reader found the place where Mordecai's act was mentioned and revealed the man had never been rewarded for his deed. Were all these details produced by coincidence, or were they evidence that God's wisdom is astonishing? Mordecai would have appreciated the words of William Cowper:

> Ye fearful saints, fresh courage take;
> The clouds ye so much dread
> Are big with mercy, and shall break
> In blessing on your head.

The Rich Rewarded . . . *Unequalled*

"And Mordecai went out from the presence of the king in royal apparel of blue and white, and with a great crown of gold, and with a garment of fine linen and purple: and the city of Shushan rejoiced and was glad" (Esther 8:15). "For Mordecai was great in the king's house, and his fame went out throughout all the provinces: for this man Mordecai waxed greater and greater" (Esther 9:4).

Adversity has always been a testing ground for oppressed saints. Recurring problems suggest that God sometimes forgets those who trust Him. Daniel might have questioned the wisdom of his being allowed to be thrown into the lions' den, and the disciples when their boat was about to capsize, asked, "Master, carest thou not that we perish?" Throughout his life David became despondent and asked, "Why art thou cast down, O my soul? and why art thou disquieted in me?" (Ps. 42:5). Shells found in the depth of the sea are much more valuable than specimens washed up on a beach. Truths learned in human grief and suffering outshine anything discovered elsewhere. Esther and Mordecai would have appreciated the words of Solomon, who wrote, "But the path of the just is as the shining light, that shineth more and more unto the perfect day" (Prov. 4:18).

MORDECAI, THE INSIGNIFICANT
JEW WHO BECAME A BIG MAN

"Now in Shushan the palace there was a certain Jew, whose name was Mordecai" (Esther 2:5).

Probably one of the most celebrated Jews mentioned in the Bible was Mordecai who sat in the gateway of Shushan, the capital city of the Persian empire. The writings of David describe many warriors who became famous because of their military exploits. The Bible also tells of Solomon and other notabilities whose wisdom was recognized internationally. Nehemiah and Ezra were patriots whose fervor inspired the returning captives to build the walls of their ransacked city. Samson took the jaw bone of an ass and overwhelmed a host of Philistines. The heroes of Israel were innumerable, but it is extremely doubtful whether any of them surpassed the Jew who every day sat in the gateway of Shushan. His fortitude was outstanding; he was a man who kept his head by using it!

Love Overcoming Loneliness

"And he brought up Hadassah, that is, Esther, his uncle's daughter: for she had neither father nor mother, and the maid was fair and beautiful; whom Mordecai, when her father and mother were dead, took for his own daughter" (Esther 2:7). On three different occasions Jews were taken as prisoners to Babylon, and at some time during that difficult period the parents of Mordecai's cousin died, leaving their child an orphan. Her age was not revealed, but it seems she was much younger than the man who welcomed her to his heart and home. Mordecai was himself a captive, but it appears he had gained favor with his captors for he "sat in the gate." That term was used to describe citizens who occupied a prominent place where people could seek their counsel. When Mordecai became aware of the plight of his cousin, he decided to adopt her into his family. Self interests were forgotten; his love for the defenseless orphan overcame any reluctance to add her to his family. That was the greatest thing he ever did. People who care for others are not forgotten either by God or men.

Help Overcoming Hatred

Mordecai was a captive from Jerusalem; one whom Nebuchadnezzar, the king of Babylon, had carried away (see Esther 2:6).

"Two of the king's chamberlains . . . sought to lay hand on the king Ahasuerus. And the thing was known to Mordecai, who told it unto Esther the queen" (Esther 2:21–22). Although a new king had begun to reign after the defeat of Nebuchadnezzar, Mordecai could have been bitter. He had lost his home and country. It is difficult to forget injustice, and the chance to gloat over the discomfiture of enemies is hard to ignore. The plot against the king had become known, and sitting at the gate, Mordecai listened to whispers concerning the insurrection. Many men would have remained silent, believing the king deserved to die. Why should a Jew protect a man who delighted in enslaving human beings? Mordecai had no ulterior motive when he spoke of the conspiracy. He resembled the Savior who taught it was wise and good to love enemies.

Faith Overcoming Fear

"And all the king's servants that were in the king's gate, bowed, and reverenced Haman: for the king had so commanded concerning him, But Mordecai bowed not, nor did him reverence" (Esther 3:2). The refusal of the Jew to obey the royal command increased the animosity of the offended nobleman, but nothing could have persuaded Mordecai to change his behavior. He reverenced only God, and to bow in adoration before a man would have been sacrilege. Mordecai may have been little of stature, but in the sight of Jehovah he was as tall as a giant!

God was never mentioned in the book of Esther, but His handiwork is seen throughout the account. His presence is never far from a soul whose integrity remains unsullied. That wonderful Hebrew was surrounded by formidable enemies, but he despised their strength. Happy and wise are all people who learn from his example. When the three young men in Babylon refused to bow before the king's idol and were thrown into the fiery furnace, they discovered the Son of God was already there awaiting their arrival. Life at times may be complex and the outlook forbidding and bleak, but always, somewhere in the shadows stands the Lord.

Trust Overcoming Terror

"When Mordecai perceived all that was done, Mordecai rent his clothes, and put on sackcloth with ashes, and went out into the midst of the city, and cried with a loud and bitter cry" (Esther 4:1). Although religion appears to be absent from the book of Esther, it is worthy of attention that the wearing of sackcloth and ashes was a sign of grief and repentance; that an offender sought mercy from God or some person with great authority.

After Israel conquered the armies of Syria, "Benhadad fled, and came into the city, into an inner chamber. And his servants said unto him, Behold now, we have heard that the kings of the house of Israel are merciful kings; let us, I pray thee, put sackcloth on our loins, and ropes upon our heads, and go out to the king of Israel: peradventure he will save thy life" (1 Kings 20:30–31).

It was evident that Mordecai never sought forgiveness from the king, and since the Persians were hostile, no effort was made to placate them. The wearing of sackcloth and ashes was meant to attract the attention of the Almighty, the Jews' only hope of survival. This man would have been less than human had he not been afraid, but beyond the problems, he saw the Lord for whom no task was impossible. The immediate future appeared to be threatening, but deep within the soul of this indomitable leader was an unshakable faith in the God of his fathers. He was a wise man.

Praise Overcoming Prejudice

"And Mordecai went out from the presence of the king in royal apparel of blue and white, and with a great crown of gold, and a garment of fine linen and purple: and the city of Shushan rejoiced and was glad. The Jews had light, and gladness, and joy, and honor. And in every province and in every city, whithersoever the king's commandment and his decree came, the Jews had joy and gladness, a feast and a good day. And many of the people of the land became Jews; for the fear of the Jews fell upon them" (Esther 8:15–17). The far-reaching conquest of the Jewish people was unmistakable, but it should be remembered the times in which these things happened were different from today. Survival was a necessity, and the threatened Hebrews were determined their problems would not be renewed. The slaughter of the Persians may seem to be merciless and regrettable, but it is interesting to note the victors never touched either money or property which belonged to their enemies. When the book of Esther was written, its author emphasized the fact the Jews were not religious mercenaries who fought to increase their wealth. They struggled for the right to exist, and that probably explains the importance of the Feast of Purim which is celebrated annually by the modern Israelis.

The fear of their conquerors fell upon the Persians, "and many of the people of the land became Jews." Even their inherent prejudices were overcome; they desired to be associated with the Hebrews, for it was evident they were a nation destined to become great.

Humility Overcoming Haughtiness

"For Mordecai the Jew was next unto king Ahasuerus, and great among the Jews, and accepted of the multitude of his brethren, seeking the wealth of his people, and speaking peace to all his seed" (Esther 10:3).

The road which led from captivity to conquest, from poverty to power was long and had many turns. When Mordecai became a prisoner of Nebuchadnezzar, his outlook was desolate. It might have been easy to believe Jehovah had forgotten to be gracious. Yet even in the darkest hour God was arranging that preservation and happiness would be possible not only for Mordecai but also for the people he represented. Some men are more faithful to God when they are in trouble. Few can overcome the temptation of being great. A bestowal of power may lead to arrogance, insensitivity, and dominating dictatorial oppression. Hitler was a little man who became important, and the world suffered because of his continuing lust for superiority. Mordecai was a different kind of man. His greatness promoted humility.

This dedicated Jew lived to increase the happiness of other people, worked for their prosperity, and cared nothing for personal gain. In spite of the destruction of his enemies he delighted in "speaking peace to all his seed" (Esther 10:3). It is not difficult to understand why the Almighty used him to be the Savior of his people. The Lord said, "Whosoever will be great among you, let him be your minister; And whosoever will be chief among you, let him be your servant" (Matt. 20:26–27).

The Great Physician Who Made House Calls

If I could relive my life and were compelled to change my occupation, I would become a doctor, for I have learned that the greatest satisfaction comes through helping other people. Yet, if that possibility ever occurred, I would be confronted by a problem. What kind of a doctor would I want to be? When I was a child in Wales, the people in our village only knew one kind of physician—the family doctor who knew something about everything! He extracted teeth, sometimes without an anaesthetic. If there was pain in any part of the body, he was expected to remove it. Occasionally when the problem was too great, patients such as I were sent to the city to consult with a specialist. There I saw an ominous chair and table, all kinds of glittering instruments, and a frightening man in a long white coat. I preferred the other doctor who practiced in the valley where I lived. Later, I discovered in California that, for the most part, the family doctor had almost become a part of history. Within the United States most medical doctors are specialists, and physicians do not infringe on the territory of a colleague. Prior to any personal consultation, forms have to be scrutinized and questions answered, and it would be easy to believe that doctors know more about their patients than the folk know about themselves. As a general rule, American physicians do not make house calls; patients are expected to visit the doctor's office where examinations are made. Jesus, who has been called the Great Physician, lived in a different age. He had no office in which to meet people, but He made at least ten house calls.

It is thought-provoking that after three and a half years of the most sensational ministry exercised among people, Zacchaeus sought to see "Jesus, *who he was*." It might be assumed that every person in the country was aware of the identity of the Savior. If this tax-gatherer was unaware of the Lord's reputation, it must be concluded he had confined himself to a world of seclusion. He was the chief of the custom officers and was detested by his countrymen. The official not only collected taxes, he applied pressure to less enthusiastic officials. The statement that said "he was rich" might imply the Romans paid high wages for his services, but the man supplemented his income by extortion. He possessed a beautiful home, but his outlook on life was biased.

Leaving his office one morning, Zacchaeus was jostled by a large crowd of people who said Jesus of Nazareth was approaching. The information aroused curiosity, and since he was unable to see over the heads of the bystanders, he climbed into a tree where his view would be unobstructed. His amazement increased when the great Physician revealed He was about to make a housecall. The Lord saw the man in the tree and said, "Zacchaeus, make haste, and come down; for to day I must abide at thy house." The ancient story reveals details which invite attention.

His Startling Wisdom . . . *Christ knew the publican's name*

"And when Jesus came to the place, he looked up and saw him, and said unto him, Zacchaeus, make haste, and come down; for today I must abide at thy house" (Luke 19:5). It was remarkable that Jesus knew the stranger's name; they had never previously met. It might be suggested that seeing the man in the tree, Jesus asked questions about him and was told he was an official named Zacchaeus. That idea, though possible, would hardly be conclusive. It seems evident the decision to visit that particular home had already been made by the Savior.

It is interesting to compare this fact with the Lord's statement, "*He calleth his own sheep by name*, and leadeth them out" (John 10:3). Expositors do not agree in their interpretation of the moral standards of the publican. Jesus referred to Zacchaeus as being a child of Abraham, and that implied he was a citizen with outstanding faith. Maybe the publican was a man of integrity, an honest and just official. Perhaps there is a similarity between this incident and the testimony of Job who said, "But *he knoweth the way that I take*: when he hath tried me, I shall come forth as gold" (Job 23:10). The Savior assured His followers that "The very hairs of your head are all numbered" (Matt. 10:30). That statement suggests God has intimate knowledge of all people whose trust He enjoys. If Christ knew about Zacchaeus, He knows about everybody.

His Sincere Wish . . . *To enter the publican's home*

"And when Jesus came to the place, he looked up, and saw him, and said unto him, Zacchaeus, make haste, and come down; for to day *I must abide at thy house*." This was one of the most surprising statements ever made by the Savior. As far as is known, it was the only occasion He invited Himself to supper in another person's home. There were other people in Jericho who had reason to be grateful to the Lord; for He had given sight to the blind, but apparently He was never invited to enter another residence. It would be extremely interesting to know why Christ was anxious to enter the publican's house. Evidently His association with Zacchaeus did not terminate when the little man descended from the branches of the sycamore tree. It was never revealed what happened within the home, but it is certain the conversation begun in the street was continued inside the dwelling. Did Christ commend the man for his faith and encourage continuance in dedicated service? Did His actions that day have any connection with John's comprehensive statement which declared, "And there are also many other things which Jesus did, the which, if they should be written every one, I suppose that even the world itself could not contain the books that should be written" (John 21:25).

The critical Pharisees would not have emulated the publican's example. "And when they saw it, they all murmured, saying, That he was gone to be a guest with a man that is a sinner" (Luke 19:7) Maybe the Lord's action was an indirect comment on the question asked by the patriarch, "If God be for us, who can be against us?" Perhaps the outstanding lesson taught in the story is that the Savior desires to become increasingly acquainted with His followers, that a man's conversion should be followed by his consecration and communion. The presence of the Lord can transform any building into a sanctuary.

His Superb Welcome . . . *"And . . . he received him joyfully"*

No person ever received the Savior *sadly*, nevertheless it was remarkable that the taxgatherer who had never before met the Lord, should respond eagerly to the Stranger in the street.

It is not known whether Zacchaeus was a married man. If he was, then his wife was about to have the greatest surprise of her life. She would not only be expected to supply a meal for Jesus but obliged, at a moment's notice, to feed the men who accompanied Him. The wealthy publican would experience no difficulty in obtaining supplies, but the unexpected guests would certainly cause embarrassment. Problems which might have seemed insurmountable to other people did not exist for the delighted host. At that moment he would have gladly fed a multitude. He had found a happiness that money could not buy. No theological doctrines had been mentioned by the Visitor; religion, repentance, morality, and other related matters did not enter into the conversation. The eyes of the taxgatherer were focused upon the Savior, and nothing else was important except to descend the tree immediately.

Blessed is the man who can say:

> What matters where on earth we dwell?
> On mountain top or in the dell:
> In cottage or a mansion fair,
> Where Jesus is, 'tis heaven there.

C. J. Butler

The outstanding feature about the New Testament church and its members was the centrality of Christ in the message proclaimed and in the hearts of the preachers. Everything uttered related to the Lord Jesus. Unfortunately, that is not true today. Strange doctrines and practices have appeared within denominations, and the Savior is excluded from the comments of some orators. On a fountain in Pontypridd, Wales, is an inscription which reads, "With Christ, we have everything; Without Christ, we have nothing."

His Splendid Work . . . *"I give to the poor . . . I restore . . . forefold"*

Throughout the history of the Christian church theologians have debated concerning the interpretation of the testimony of Zacchaeus. He said to the Lord, "Behold, Lord, the half of my goods I give to the poor; and if I have taken any thing from any man by false accusation, I restore him fourfold." The Greek Testament interprets the statement as it is found in the King James Version of the Scriptures. The Amplified Bible inserts the word (now) to make the statement, "See, Lord, the half of my goods I (now) give (by way of restoration) to the poor; and if I have cheated anyone out of anything, I (now) restore him four times as much." There is flexibility in this translation, but it is not conclusive that Zacchaeus suddenly amended his ways.

Had he been an extortionist or irreligious he may not have been conversant with the laws of Moses. Three times within the Pentateuch the patriarch gave instructions regarding reparations (see Ex. 22:1, Lev. 6:5, Num. 5:6–7). The publican did not say, "I will restore him fourfold." His words suggest this was his daily practice; that he was an honorable man trying to live an exemplary life in difficult circumstances. Arguments may be advanced in favor of both interpretations, but the impact of the Lord upon the publican was undeniable. Paul wrote to the Corinthians stating, "Therefore if any man be in Christ, he is a new creature: old things are passed away; behold, all things are become new" (2 Cor. 5:17). When a person looks into the face of Jesus, sermons are unnecessary to accomplish what needs to be done.

His Suggestive Witness . . . *"He also is a son of Abraham"*

It might be affirmed that all Jews were sons of Abraham, but salvation did not come to every Hebrew home. Luke described an incident in the synagogue when Christ referred to "a daughter of Abraham" and where, in all probability, the Lord was emphasizing that any descendant of the Patriarch deserved to be helped (see Luke 13:16). The woman was bowed down with a great infirmity. Zacchaeus, as far as is known, did not suffer from any sickness. He was wealthy and in good health and apparently content with his position in life. He desired to know more of the Man whose ministry had challenged the nation. If, as has been suggested, he was a pious man endeavoring to live according to the laws of the Almighty, then his religion had brought him to the edge of reality. When he discovered all he required was in Christ, happiness overwhelmed his soul.

It may be impossible to decide authoritatively the spiritual state of the publican's soul, but it became evident that Jesus desired to present him a treasure of incalculable worth. It would be informative to know the rest of the story of Zacchaeus. People had seemed to be giants when they interfered with his view of the Lord, but actually they were ordinary men and women. The taxgatherer had been so obsessed with his problem, he overlooked the fact that he was small—the trouble was within himself. No tree is too tall to climb when sincere souls are determined to see the Savior. When the great Physician finally terminated that house call, He had ministered to one of His most famous patients.

The feast held in the home of the Pharisee presents problems. Why did Simon invite Jesus into his home? Was he trying to enhance his reputation as a generous host? There were others who dined with him (see Luke 7:49). Was he hoping to expose violations of Hebrew law regarding the washing of hands before meals? He believed Jesus might be a prophet, but was he hoping to learn more during the meal? His early condemnation of the Savior revealed a need of understanding and concern. He was a typical Pharisee whose life was dominated by tradition.

The appearance of the immoral woman was not surprising, for the presence of such people was welcomed at functions where guests desired illicit entertainment. That unexpected visitor did certain things destined to make her famous: (1) she came with a gift, (2) stood behind him weeping, (3) washed His feet with her tears, (4) wiped them with her hair, (5) kissed His feet, and (6) anointed His feet with ointment.

Her Reputation . . . *How Condemned*

Apparently this woman was a lady of the night who earned a living by breaking the heart of God. She had evidently invested some of her money in precious ointment which she hoped would increase her attractiveness. It supplied aroma which lured customers into moral degradation. Nothing was recorded to explain her first contact with the Savior, therefore it must be assumed she had attended one of His open-air meetings where her life was transformed. His message illuminated the dark recesses of her soul, and forgetting other people, she was condemned by her conscience. It is interesting that she and the proud Pharisee were brought together by Luke to provide an illuminating contrast. Simon the Pharisee was proud, pitiable, and popular, the woman was defiled, disturbed, and determined. Yet the woman had a far better chance of being forgiven than the self-confident host.

Her Resolve . . . *How Concerned*

Perhaps this woman had listened to Jesus and had gone away troubled. If that were true, she returned later to discover the Preacher was being entertained in a nearby home. The Bible says, "When she knew that Jesus sat at meat in the Pharisee's house . . ." Evidently, the woman made inquiries and was told of the invitation given by Simon. That could have hindered an ordinary person, but this lady earnestly desired to meet the Preacher and was ready to overcome any obstacle preventing that achievement. Her appearance in Simon's home had far-reaching repercussions. It was not difficult to gain admittance to the home; she might even have been there earlier!

Her Repentance . . . *How Convincing*

Simon, who was haughty, proud, and self-confident, expressed no surprise when the woman unceremoniously entered, and even his criticism of Christ was not audibly heard. "He spake within himself." The woman looked around, recognized the Lord, and walking toward Him, "stood at his feet behind him weeping." It was doubtful whether she had ever wept in the presence of men. Laughter was the hallmark of her trade, but her attitude had changed. She felt unclean, unwanted, and undeserving of favor. There was great similarity between this episode and another which told of Christ's visit to the home of Simon the leper. There were two Simons, two women, and two boxes of very precious ointment. One woman came to Christ because of her defilement; Mary came because of her devotion. The one Simon invited the Lord to supper because of unrevealed reasons. The other welcomed the Lord because he desired to pay a debt of love owed to his Savior. The woman's tears revealed the sorrow filling the soul of a penitent woman who was morally bankrupt.

Her Regeneration . . . *How Complete*

"She kissed his feet and anointed them with the ointment." When that treasure was purchased, she had no idea how it would ultimately be used. She hoped it would increase her attractiveness, but the meeting with Jesus of Nazareth changed her plans. Indiscretion and failure terminated when a new life began. She would never need that kind of adornment again; the box of perfume was given to Jesus as evidence of a new commitment. Paul was correct when he wrote, "If any man [or woman] be in Christ, he [or she] is a new creature; old things are passed away; behold, all things are become new" (2 Cor. 5:17).

"Now when the Pharisee which had bidden him saw it, he spake within himself, saying, This man, *if he were a prophet*, would have known who and what manner of woman this is that toucheth him:

for she is a sinner" (Luke 7:39). When Simon watched from the head of the table, his eyes had become speculative. He had considered the possibility that Jesus was some kind of a prophet but evidently did not believe compassion, kindness, and tenderness were attributes of God's chosen servants. He had his own ideas concerning what was right or wrong and appointed himself judge of his Guest.

The message concerning the creditor who had two debtors destroyed Simon's conceit. Jesus spoke of two men who owed five hundred and fifty pence respectively. Both were forgiven, but the Lord asked, "Tell me therefore, which of them will love him most?" Simon's answer revealed embarrassment, for he answered: "I suppose he, to whom he forgave most." Probably the Lord smiled when He replied, "Thou hast rightly judged. And he turned to the woman and said unto Simon: Seest thou this woman? I entered into thine house, thou gavest me no water for my feet; but she hath washed my feet with tears, and wiped them with the hairs of her head. Thou gavest me no kiss: but this woman since the time I came hath not ceased to kiss my feet. My head with oil thou didst not anoint: but this woman hath anointed my feet with ointment. Wherefore I say unto thee, Her sins which are many are forgiven; for she loved much: but to whom little is forgiven, the same loveth little. And he said unto her, Thy sins are forgiven" (Luke 7:43–48).

The phrase "since the time I came in" might suggest the woman was within the Pharisee's home even before the arrival of the Lord. Her repentance and love were manifest as soon as Jesus entered. If that were true, then the Savior planned two things when He accepted Simon's invitation. He desired to rescue a woman from evil and at the same time deliver a message to the Pharisee and his guests. The interpretation of the earlier verse presents another problem. Did the Lord find the woman, or did she find Him?

An elderly man, recently converted, was taunted by his companion who said, "Sam, they tell me that last night you found Jesus." The man replied, "No George, I didn't find Jesus—He found me."

Her Redeemer . . . *How Compassionate*

Sometimes white lilies emerge from the filthiest of ponds, and this was so when a redeemed woman forsook the repulsiveness of her profession. She listened to every word uttered by the Lord, and the impact upon her soul became evident.

(1) *How Different!* When the Pharisee saw the woman anointing the Lord with ointment, he murmured disdainfully, "This man, if he were a prophet, would have known what manner of woman this is that toucheth him: for she is a sinner." It would not have mattered what she did, the critical host would have condemned her. Yet Jesus, the chief guest, was kind, sympathetic, and loving. The warmth of His compassion brought hope to her despondent soul. He made her feel that God loved her, that her sins could be forgiven. The Pharisee represented relentless laws, but the Lord was introducing a new way of helping people in need. "For the law was given by Moses [and misinterpreted by the Pharisees], but grace and truth came by Jesus Christ" (John 1:17).

(2) *How Definite!* It was said of the Savior that "he taught them as one having authority, and not as the scribes" (Matt. 7:29). That fact was emphasized during the supper in Simon's house. Christ's defense of the woman was remarkably effective. When He contrasted the host's hospitality with the attitude of the repentant sinner, the impact upon the proud Pharisee was unmistakable. Jesus concluded His remarks by saying, "Wherefore I say unto thee, Her sins, which are many, are forgiven; for she loved much" (Luke 7:47). This was a direct contradiction of the teaching of the Pharisees who taught that pardon was the reward of endeavor. Sinners were required to work their way into the favor of God. Jesus rejected that doctrine and insisted that love for God was better than sacrifices. He endorsed the words of David who said, "For thou desirest not sacrifice; else would I give it: thou delightest not in burnt offering. The sacrifices of God are a broken spirit: a broken and a contrite heart, O God, thou wilt not despise" (Ps. 51:16–17). David, the king of Israel, looked into his own soul and trembled; the woman looked into the face of Jesus and believed.

(3) *How Discerning!* The Pharisee remembered her evil reputation. Christ saw what she could become and said, "Thy faith hath saved thee" (Luke 7:50). She had not complied with any of the laws related to repentance and sacrifice, and as far as is known, was not even religiously inclined. She was an unfortunate sinner struggling to survive amid circumstances which threatened to destroy her soul. Simon believed he was pleasing God; the woman hardly knew where she was until she met Jesus. The listeners at the supper quickly recognized the Lord's claim to be unique. They said, "Who

104

is this that forgiveth sins also?" They were evidently aware of His reputation as a healer, but even miracles were less important than His ability to pardon sin. They believed that only God had the authority and power to forgive transgressions. At a later date the religious leaders accused Jesus, saying, "This man maketh himself equal with God." Describing that incident, John wrote, "Therefore the Jews sought the more to kill him, because he not only had broken the sabbath, but said also that God was his Father, making himself equal with God" (John 5:18). While the people in Simon's house considered this matter, the Lord saw a precious soul emerging from degradation. His words, "Thy faith hath saved thee" could have great depths of meaning. Was He suggesting that in addition to being saved from immorality, she was being delivered eternally from the consequences of evil?

(4) *How Delightful!* "Go in peace." Apparently Jesus often used these words, for He repeated them when speaking to the woman who touched the hem of His garment (see Luke 8:48). All people who have received pardon from the Lord should "*go in peace*"— and never worry about former indiscretions. When God forgives, He forgets. He said, "I will forgive their iniquity, and I will remember their sin no more" (Jer. 31:34). If God has buried sins in the sea of forgetfulness, Christians should leave them there! To resurrect former mistakes and worry about them is to destroy the peace that should fill the souls of all believers. Since God has forgotten our sins, we should emulate His example.

Perhaps one of the pleasures in eternity will be listening to this woman's testimony. We have no information about anything that happened after her departure from the home of the Pharisee. Did she marry or seek new employment? Was she ever tempted to return to her former occupation, and did she overcome as she remembered her meeting with the Savior? Jesus said He came into the world to save sinners. The woman would have appreciated that statement. Had He not entered into the home of Simon to save her? The great Physician had transformed a part of the Pharisee's house into a consulting room where perfect health was restored to her ailing soul.

THE HOME IN CANA—TO SHOW
HIS SPLENDOR (JOHN 2:1–11)

Christians would like to know more of the bridal couple who invited Jesus to their wedding. Were they young or middle-aged, relatives or neighbors of Mary, and why did they include the disciples who probably were strangers? John wrote, "And the third day there was a marriage in Cana of Galilee; and the mother of Jesus was there." She did not need an invitation! That fact invited investigation, for evidently Mary was not a guest. Today such a person would either be a caterer, a coordinator in charge of proceedings, or a reporter authorized to collect facts and take photographs for publication or family pleasure. The fact that Mary's presence was announced without explanation might indicate she was a trusted and loyal friend of one of the families. Either the bride, the groom, or both, wanted her to share their special day.

If Mary was an intimate friend or relative of the family, it may be assumed the couple also knew Jesus. He was known to be a carpenter, who perhaps had already made a wedding gift for the bride and groom. Marriages in Palestine were celebrated by festivities that continued for several days, and guests were invited to stay as long as possible. At that time Jesus had four disciples; Andrew, Simon, Philip, and Nathaniel, who also were "called to the wedding" (see John 1:40, 47–49). Jesus and His followers appeared to be inseparable, but it is not known if Mary had any part in inviting additional guests.

John's description of the wedding was significant. He believed that during the proceedings Jesus "manifested forth his glory" (John 2:11). The happy bride and groom were not aware of the fact, but their wedding had been planned in heaven before they were born. Jesus had already decided to use the occasion to reveal the glory He shared with His Father before time began (see John 17:5). The Lord had not previously been the great Physician. He was more like a graduate from God's School of Medicine about to embark upon a career, meeting His first patients. Circumstances were about to destroy the happiness of two special people, but the Savior intervened to make the event a very memorable occasion.

Many problems perplex Christians, but blessed are they who share their emergencies with the Son of God. When Jesus solved the problem at the wedding, it became evident He always gave more than He received. No home was impoverished when He was there.

His Presence Was Requested . . . *A Gracious Desire*

What might have happened if the Savior had not been present at that wedding? Thrills would have been replaced by embarrassment and delights by disappointments. The neighbors would have remembered the lack of wine rather than the love of a woman. It is commendable when believers invite the Lord to share their sorrow, but it is even more so when Christ is invited—not for what He might give, but for what He might receive from us. Jesus was pleased to give His benediction to those about to be joined in matrimony. Many years have passed since that memorable occasion, but He has not changed. He said, "For where two or three are gathered together in my name, there am I in the midst of them" (Matt. 18:20). Tertullian, one of the early church leaders, believed that promise related to the Christian family. He interpreted the statement as "When two (the husband and wife) or three (their child) are met together in my name, there am I in the midst of them." All young people should remember that Jesus loves to attend weddings.

Unless a marriage is solemnized in the presence of Christ and thereafter life revolves around Him, the union may quickly deteriorate. It is a cause for regret that many modern marriages end within months. When the fascination of wedlock wears off and participants become attracted to others, matrimonial vows are quickly forgotten. Young people see no need for wedding ceremonies and are content to live together. They believe the money saved can be used to furnish a home. If their marriage fails, they can separate and save the money necessary to make divorce legal! This indicates moral decay within a nation. When parents pray with their children, the danger of disintegration within the family is minimized, and the future filled with prospect and hope. Conversion follows when people invite Christ into their hearts. Contentment is preserved when the Savior is given first place in their homes. The couple in Cana of Galilee recognized this fact, and Jesus probably was high on the list of friends invited to the marriage.

His Power Was Recognized . . . *A Great Discernment*

It should be remembered that prior to this wedding, as far as is known, Jesus had not performed any public miracles. Mary had

107

lived with Him for thirty years, and what she witnessed enabled her to believe the Lord could do the impossible. When she became aware of the predicament in the kitchen, she hastened to Jesus to share the news of the embarrassing situation. Although He made no promise to intervene, she looked into His eyes and was assured He could not remain indifferent to the problem. Her statement to the servants was inspired by faith. She said, "Whatsoever he saith unto you, do it" (John 2:5). Her range of possibilities defied limitation. Had the Lord commanded the most outrageous thing, Mary, though puzzled, would have said, "*do it*." Faith and doubt cannot live together; one will destroy the other.

Mary believed her Son could do the impossible, but He needed human cooperation. Obedience is the introduction to overcoming. When the servants had filled the pots, the water in the well became wine, and they continued to draw until every need was supplied. If they had ceased their efforts, guests would have remained thirsty. God placed wine in the well, but the servants had to take it out. The great Physician may supply medicine, but His patients must take it!

Many years later when John reminisced and described that first miracle, he said, "This beginning of miracles did Jesus in Cana of Galilee, and manifested forth his glory" (John 2:11). The author of the first gospel saw in the event much more than the solving of a temporary problem. He saw this display as an indescribable attribute which Jesus had from eternity. The Lord possessed something which He shared with God from earth's earliest ages. The word glory is a diamond with many facets. It might be expressed as excellence, majesty, brightness, or effulgence. It is impossible to comprehend everything about God, but whatever is found in the Almighty can be seen in the Lord Jesus Christ. John believed this display of everlasting excellence was visible during the wedding in Cana.

The apostle suggested that Mary alone was aware of this possibility. She knew beforehand what He was able to accomplish. They had lived in the same home for thirty years, and what she saw during that time influenced her outlook. Her Son was capable of doing the impossible. When the governor of the feast praised the quality of the wine, Mary quietly said, "I knew He could do it." Faith brings its own reward. No one can live close to Jesus and remain unaware of His capabilities.

"When the ruler of the feast had tasted the water that was made wine, and knew not whence it was: (but the servants which drew the water knew;) the governor of the feast called the bridegroom, And saith unto him, Every man at the beginning doth set forth good wine; and when men have well drunk, then that which is worse: but thou hast kept the good wine until now" (John 2:9–10). Three details deserve consideration.

(1) The Pertinent Question. The logic of the governor's comment should be a warning to all alcoholics. It drew attention to the indisputable fact that when men "have well drunk" their minds cannot differentiate between good and evil; even cheap liquor may seem an excellent vintage. The ruler of the feast, who probably had supervised many wedding receptions, instantly recognized the difference in procedure. For some inscrutable reason, the best wine was now inferior. This new refreshment presented to the guests superseded anything produced by the local wineries. The governor was amazed and desired to know why the usual custom had been reversed. Unaware of the miracle, he could not be expected to know that anything supplied by the Savior surpassed everything produced by man.

(2) The Pleasing Quality. "Thou hast kept the good wine until now." It has been reported that when John Wesley was a student, he was required to write about the miracle at Cana. His mind would not respond and, with only a few moments left, Wesley wrote, "The wine looked at Jesus and blushed." The human mind is unable to comprehend the unlimited power of the Lord; how He changed the water into wine is as mystifying as how He placed billions of worlds in space. Yet one thing is evident—His wine was not fermented. It was the pure juice of grapes, something which would never impair the faculties of men and women. When Peter and his colleagues preached on the day of Pentecost, the people "were all amazed, and were in doubt, saying one to another, what meaneth this? Others mocking said: These men are full of new wine. But Peter, standing up with the eleven, lifted up his voice, and said unto them, Ye men of Judaea, and all ye that dwell at Jerusalem, Be this known unto you, and hearken to my words: For these are not drunken, as ye suppose, seeing it is but the third hour of the day" (Acts 2:12–15). That display of spiritual power was not the product of troubled minds. The preachers were not drunkards, but God-fearing citizens

who had met the risen Christ. The Holy Spirit had given them a degree of happiness which, like the wine at Cana, could only be supplied by Christ.

(3) The Perfect Quantity. Some commentators believe Jesus filled seven pots with wine. A careful consideration of the Scriptures may negate that idea. When the Savior said, "Draw out now," He might have been referring to the well which in all probability was in the courtyard of the home. The servants had already filled six large pots, for the water was used in ceremonial washings before and after meals. A firkin equals about nine gallons, and thus each container held between 18 and 27 gallons. The total capacity of the six waterpots would be approximately 140 to 150 gallons. That these were empty at this time would suggest a large number of diligent guests and an unknown number of careless servants! The men had been drawing water from the well and probably continued to do so. It is hard to believe that good wine would be wasted on ceremonial observances. Yet before the wedding terminated, more water would be needed. Possibly Jesus commanded the servants to fill the waterpots for two reasons: (1) that water would be available from the stone jars when only wine was being drawn from the well and (2) that faith is hardly faith until it is tested and proved to be true. Even the servants had to exercise faith before the miracle became a reality. The well continued to produce wine as long as it was needed; afterward everything reverted to pattern. One wonders what connection might be made between this verse and its predecessor in Isaiah 23:3, "Therefore with joy shall ye draw water out of the wells of God's salvation."

THE HOME OF SIMON—TO STRENGTHEN
A SAINT (MATTHEW 26:6–7)

"Now when Jesus was in Bethany, in the home of Simon the leper, There came unto him a woman having an alabaster box of very precious ointment, and poured it on his head as he sat at meat." Perhaps Martha was busy in her kitchen when she heard a voice saying, "May I come in?" She smiled when she saw her friend who lived down the street. She liked him, but that was not a cause for amazement; she liked everybody! Simon, who had been a leper, asked, "Is it true the Master is expected today?" His face became radiant when she replied, "Yes, Simon, Jesus will be here this afternoon." When her visitor seemed embarrassed, she asked, "What is on your mind, Simon?" He thought for a moment and then answered, "Well, Martha, you know I was a leper, and but for the Master's help I would have died. He was kind to me, and now I would like to do something for Him. I know He always stays in this house, and that is wonderful, but would you object if I invited Him to supper tonight? I am not a good cook and would appreciate your help." That gracious lady agreed to become the hostess for the forthcoming meal, and later when the Savior arrived, she whispered, "Master, You remember Simon the leper. We are going to have supper in his house tonight. It will mean so much to him for he thinks he will never be able to pay the debt he owes to You."

The name Simon was common throughout Palestine, and that led to the practice of adding something that resembled a surname. To differentiate between people bearing the same name, neighbors referred to them as Simon the tanner (see Acts 9:43); Simon the Pharisee (see Luke 7:40); Simon the leper (see Matt. 26:6). There were others such as Simon who carried the cross of Jesus and Simon the sorcerer. There has been much speculation regarding the Simon who lived in Bethany; some teachers believe he was either the husband or father of Martha. This appears to be improbable, for he lived in his own home, and it would be difficult to explain why he did not reside with his family.

It is believed this man had been a leper until he met Jesus of Nazareth. It is easy to imagine what happened on that memorable occasion and to understand why he decided to live in Bethany. He might have been a relative of Martha, Mary, and Lazarus, whose financial assistance enabled him to establish a new home. These are only possibilities, but certain facts are indisputable.

An Unsurpassable Gift . . . *An Incurable Disease*

Nothing is known about the early life of this unique man, but many theories have been expressed concerning his illness. Was he the leper who knelt before the Lord? (see Matt. 8:2). Is it possible that he was one of the ten unfortunate men who cried for mercy? (see Luke 17:12–13). Could he have been an inmate of a leper colony, and did some friend or relative intercede on his behalf? The Scriptures do not mention how, when, or where the leper was cleansed, and suggestions can only be speculative. One fact is irrefutable; the man was threatened by death until he met Jesus of Nazareth and received hope for the future. Christ was the only person able to perform that miracle—at that time there was no known cure for leprosy.

The meeting with the Savior brought new life to the sufferer. This is probably one of the most important facts revealed in the Bible. The Lord said He came into the world to save sinners. Simon Peter claimed: "Neither is there salvation in any other: for there is none other name under heaven given among men, whereby we must be saved" (Acts 4:12). Paul wrote, "The gift of God is eternal life through Jesus Christ our Lord" (Rom. 6:23). Lepers could neither save themselves nor pay for their deliverance. Their survival depended upon the ability of Jesus to respond and their determination to seek His aid. This truth cannot change. Even the greatest scientist cannot create life nor defeat death, yet the Savior did both.

An Unending Gratitude . . . *An Increasing Debt*

Memories are messengers from the past, reminders of events that might disappear into oblivion. Since Simon did not become an itinerant evangelist, it was necessary to establish a home, and after some consideration he decided to live in Bethany. If he was a friend of Martha, Mary, and Lazarus, the desire to become their neighbor was understood and appreciated. He would have liked to remain with Jesus forever, but since that was impossible, he was content to live near people who shared his love for the Lord. Every day he reminisced, and the awareness of his debt to Jesus deepened. How could he express to his Benefactor all that was within his soul? Had he been a public speaker, he would have been among the seventy

112

disciples. Had he been a younger man, many avenues of service would have been forthcoming. Unfortunately there was not much he could do. Every day Simon considered his options, but when he heard of the imminent arrival of Jesus, it seemed that his silent prayers had been answered.

He could and would invite Jesus to dinner, and if Martha would take charge of the kitchen arrangements, the forthcoming meal would be the best ever prepared. He was anxious to make that evening a time to be remembered. Within moments Simon was on his way to Martha's home. Nothing was ever recorded about the meal except that Mary anointed the head of Jesus with the expensive ointment. Simon's shining eyes were trying to tell the Master He was loved and appreciated. People who forget to return thanks are unworthy of commendation.

An Understanding Guest . . . *An Interested Deliverer*

The Lord enjoyed and appreciated the reception in the home of the former leper and watched as Martha proudly carried in what had been prepared. He was thrilled to be entertained by His friends, but it was strange that He who had used a lad's lunch to feed a multitude was pleased to receive whatever was provided by Simon. The Lord could have supplied the greatest meal ever conceived in the mind of God, for He had helped to plant the garden eastward in Eden and had created every fruit and vegetable. He was pleased to receive a love-offering from sincere friends. Simon was ecstatic, but the Lord was happier than the host.

This reflected the pattern of Christ's entire ministry. The Lord never solicited financial assistance, the disciples never received a collection in any service, and as far as is known, they were not sponsored by wealthy patrons. It was expensive to maintain their work over a period of three and a half years. The preachers needed food, and their clothing and footwear did not last forever. On one occasion in order to pay taxes Peter was sent to catch a fish that had a coin in its mouth, but never in any emergency did Jesus appeal for financial assistance. Modern evangelists do not emulate their Master's example.

Evidently some people helped to meet the need of that dedicated company, and what they gave was supervised by Judas "who kept the bag." The Lord could have provided everything necessary to maintain the smooth operation of His crusade, but He allowed people to share the responsibility of spreading the gospel. Sacrificial giving enabled men and women to develop their spirituality. They gave and discovered God always returned more than they had given. The great Physician, in visiting the home of Simon, saw improvement in His patient. The former leper was enjoying perfect health! Throughout the centuries Christ has not changed. He always gives more than He receives.

An Unmistakable Gesture . . . *An Important Duty*

If some person had asked Simon why he invited the Lord to supper, he would have probably replied, "I was compelled to invite Him. It was my inescapable duty to welcome Him into my home." People who profess to be grateful for blessing received and whose hands remain closed become misers. They are inhospitable, selfish, and unattractive. It has often been said, "It is better to give than receive," but some people never know that pleasure.

There has always been a great difference between ministering to the Lord and ministering for Him. Both aspects of Christian service are splendid, but doing something personal for Christ is the most commendable of spiritual endeavors. When Simon witnessed to his friends and neighbors about the cleansing power of the Savior, he did something *for* the Lord, thereby helping to extend His influence. When he planned that sumptuous meal, he was only concerned with the Savior's personal pleasure. Success in extending the kingdom of God is certain to attract attention and public acclaim. Pleasing the Lord may never do this, but it thrills the heart of God. Unfortunately some Christians are too busy to sit at His feet.

When Luke described the prayer meeting held in the church at Antioch, he wrote, "Now there were in the church that was at Antioch certain prophets and teachers; as Barnabas, and Simeon that was called Niger, and Lucius of Cyrene, and Manaen, which had been brought up with Herod the tetrarch, and Saul. As they ministered to the Lord, and fasted, the Holy Spirit said: Separate me Barnabas and Saul for the work whereunto I have called them" (Acts 13:1–2). All the men mentioned by Luke were ardent servants of Christ, who spent most of their time ministering within the church. They were prophets and teachers who instructed believers. Yet on this occasion the busy workers were hushed. Their eyes were focused on the Lord. They were ministering to Jesus. All preachers should kneel before the Savior before they stand before people.

Simon the leper in all probability had witnessed to neighbors on many occasions; he loved doing this *for* his Master, yet his finest hour came when, forgetting others, he completely centered his attention on Christ. Had he failed to do this, his soul would have been impoverished.

An Undiminishing Glory . . . *An Inspiring Delight*

During that memorable evening in the neighbor's home, Mary electrified the gathering when she anointed the Lord with her very precious ointment. The action aroused indignation in some of the disciples, and thereafter the warmth of Simon's hospitality was overshadowed. "There came unto him a woman having an alabaster box of very precious ointment, and poured it on his head, as he sat at meat. But when the disciples saw it, they had indignation, saying, To what purpose is this waste? For this ointment might have been sold for much, and given to the poor. When Jesus understood it, he said unto them, Why trouble ye the woman? for she hath wrought a good work upon me. . . . Verily I say unto you, Wheresoever this gospel shall be preached in the whole world, there shall also this, that this woman hath done, be told for a memorial of her" (Matt. 26:7–13). Did the criticism ruin the serenity of Simon's party? Probably frowns appeared on the faces of those who watched and listened, but unseen by many was the simple fact that Mary's act of devotion brought immortality to the kindly host. The world knows about the gift of that delightful woman, but they also know the incident happened in the home of Simon, whose soul was filled with gratitude. The Savior knew there would be innumerable people interested in expressing their thanks for blessings received, and to encourage them He said, "Then shall the King say unto them on his right hand, Come, ye blessed of my Father, inherit the kingdom prepared for you from the foundation of the world: For I was an hungered, and ye gave me meat: I was thirsty, and ye gave me drink: I was a stranger and ye took me in: Naked, and ye clothed me: I was sick, and ye visited me: I was in prison, and ye came unto me. Then shall the righteous answer him, saying, Lord, when saw we thee an hungered and fed thee? or thirsty, and gave thee drink? When saw we thee a stranger, and took thee in? or naked, and clothed thee? Or when saw we thee sick, or in prison, and came unto thee? And the King shall answer and say unto them, Verily I say unto you, Inasmuch as ye have done it unto one of the least of these my brethren, ye have done it unto me" (Matt. 25:34–40). Solomon said, "Whatsoever thy hand findeth to do, do it with all thy might; for there is no work, nor device, nor knowledge, nor wisdom, in the grave, whither thou goest" (Eccl. 9:10). The time to minister to Christ is *now*; the opportunity to win souls for His kingdom is *now*—no soul will be saved in eternity.

Jairus the ruler of the synagogue had a terrible problem; he was caught between a rock and a hard place! His authority among the Hebrew congregation was unquestioned. He had ruled with dignity and honor. Every sabbath and as often as necessary he warned his people against the heretic from Nazareth who had apparently violated Jewish laws. Nevertheless, his pride and love were in conflict. His daughter lay dangerously ill, and Jesus alone offered the prospect of recovery. If he sought aid from the Healer, his job would be in jeopardy, and critics would be merciless in their denunciation. If he refrained from antagonizing the Pharisees, he would attend the funeral of his child. It will never be known how fierce the battle was within his soul before he made an irrevocable decision.

"And, behold, there came a man named Jairus, and he was a ruler of the synagogue: and he fell down at Jesus' feet, and besought him that he would come into his house: For he had one only daughter, about twelve years of age, and she lay a dying." The need was urgent, the situation desperate, but something had interrupted the journey toward the ruler's house. A woman had touched the hem of Christ's garment, and time was being wasted! If Jesus continued to interrogate people, delay might be fatal. "While he yet spake, there cometh one from the ruler of the synagogue's house, saying to him, Thy daughter is dead; trouble not the Master." The Lord overheard the remark and said, "Fear not; believe only, and she shall be made whole" (Luke 8:49–50).

The crowd was approaching the home where the tragedy had occurred, and the professional mourners were already expressing their pseudo grief. Wails and excessive sobbing endorsed the news that the child had expired. The noise subsided when Jesus said, "Weep not; she is not dead, but sleepeth." Every person present was amazed when the cries of anguish were replaced by hysterical laughter; it was disgusting and revolting when, in the presence of grieving parents, the hypocritical minstrels "laughed him to scorn." Slowly, the Savior opened the door and asked the offensive cynics to leave. Their mirth disappeared, their job was cancelled, and the frustration and bitterness was evident to all. Yet they left, for He who had cleansed the temple and expelled the money changers was determined to enforce their departure. They did not know they were in the presence of the Lord of life. When Jesus left that home, the girl was enfolded in the arms of her mother, and the adoring father was struggling to maintain his composure. His congregation might not be sympathetic. The Pharisees would cause endless problems, but at least his daughter was alive, and nothing else was important. Once again the great Physician had made a special house call, and the little family would always be grateful.

The Difficult Decision . . . *Faith Taunted*

The writers of the Gospels said Jairus was one of the rulers of the synagogue. That could mean he was a ruler of one particular synagogue to which he belonged, or he was a member of an elite company of men who supervised Hebrew jurisprudence throughout Galilee. What remains of the burned-out synagogue in Capernaum enables visitors to understand the importance of this position. A long and conspicuous stone seat placed at the front and to the left of the congregation indicates rulers sat apart from the main audience and were regarded with esteem and honor. When circumstances demanded, these elected officials were responsible for the instruction of young people. They were in charge of the sacred rolls and responsible for the maintenance of the sanctuary. They offered advice and guidance to the community and in matters of vital importance gave counsel to individuals. Their decisions were irreversible; there was no court of appeal. All matters of internal unrest were referred to the ruling body of elders who were expected to maintain high standards of spiritual morality.

Jairus was a ruler of a synagogue, and all these conditions applied to him. When the teachings of Jesus appeared to challenge the Hebrew faith, it would have been his duty to warn the congregation of consequences which followed heresy. No one ever questioned the sincerity of the man whose child was known throughout the area. When the girl was threatened by death, her father was placed in a very difficult situation. It was not easy to forget the advice he had given to others, but it was terrible to watch the suffering of his adored child. How could he seek assistance from Jesus when his congregation remembered his earlier denunciations? It was exceptionally hard to decide what he should do. He either had to preserve his honor or lose his child. The rich young ruler chose between wealth and discipleship and refused to abandon his money. The ruler of the synagogue was forced to choose between his child and local popularity. The world now knows the daughter was raised because her father knelt! "He fell down at Jesus' feet, and besought him that he would come into his house" (Luke 8:41).

A Disturbing Delay . . . *Faith Tested*

Language could never express the ruler's happiness when Jesus granted his request. He wanted to run all the way home. When the party came to a halt, the man wondered why Jesus had paused on the roadway. "And a woman having an issue of blood twelve years, which had spent all her living upon physicians, neither could be healed of any, Came behind him, and touched the border of his garment: and immediately her issue of blood staunched. And Jesus said, Who touched me? When all denied, Peter and they that were with him said, Master, the multitude throng thee and press thee, and sayest thou, Who touched me? And Jesus said, Somebody hath touched me: for I perceive that virtue is gone out of me" (Luke 8:43–46).

Possibly the Lord only paused for a few minutes, but to the worried parent the delay seemed endless. Why could not that woman have chosen another time to seek assistance? His daughter was dying; the need was critical and urgent. What if she expired before the Healer arrived? During those terrible moments the faith of that father was severely tested. Then the dreaded event happened. "While he yet spake, there cometh one from the ruler of the synagogue's house, saying to him, Thy daughter is dead; trouble not the Master" (Luke 8:49).

During such moments doubt sometimes overwhelms the soul. When clouds fill the sky, it is easy to forget the sun continues to shine. The man was exceedingly anxious, "But when Jesus heard it, he answered him, saying, Fear not: believe only, and she shall be made whole" (Luke 8:50). All the miracles of the Savior carried His hallmark of kindness. Had he hastened to the home of Jairus, an impoverished woman would have been denied the pleasure of meeting her greatest Benefactor. Even the delays of the Lord are proof of His care. Circumstances may suggest God is sometimes forgetful, but in moments of distress He is never far away.

The Deadly Distraction . . . *Faith Threatened*

They had reached the street in which Jairus resided, and the unusual noise indicated tragedy had devastated one of the homes. The mourners who were always hired for such events were already at work; their wails of grief echoed through the street, and people were listening and waiting to see anything spectacular. Describing the scene, Matthew wrote, "And when Jesus came into the ruler's house, and saw the minstrels and the people making a noise . . ." (see Matt. 9:23).

"In the later part of the Old Testament paid professional mourners, generally female, take an important place in the mourning rituals. Known as 'mourning women' or 'skillful women' (see Jer. 9:17), 'cunning women' or as 'singing women' (see 2 Chron. 35:25), these individuals embellished the funeral rites with skillfully contrived dirges and eulogies (see Amos 5:16). Sometimes they were accompanied by flutes. Their office was passed on from mother to daughter (see Jer. 9:20)" *The Zondervan Encyclopedia of the Bible,* vol. 4 (Grand Rapids: Zondervan Publishing House, 1976), p. 306.

These people who were completely insensitive to the grief of the family listened to the words of Jesus and laughed him to scorn. It was disgusting that they filled a house of sadness with hysterical mirth. It may never be known whether payment was made for their abominable performance, for before they could complete the dirges, the Savior expelled them. Throughout those tragic moments the troubled Jairus listened and watched. Maybe earlier fears returned to ask, "What will happen if Jesus cannot do what I require? What will my colleagues say and think if after all this my daughter is buried?" The Lord was aware of those fears. "For he knoweth our frame; he remembereth that we are dust" (Ps. 103:14). God never whips His children in an effort to make them follow Him; He prefers to hold out His arms and say, "Come unto me, all ye that labor and are heavy laden, and I will give you rest" (Matt. 11:28). Christ knows when faith is being tested; when danger surrounds us, "underneath are the everlasting arms." Probably the Lord expelled the scorners, "But when he had put them all out" (Mark 5:40), because He desired to safeguard the future of the ruler. Later "he charged them straitly that no man should know it; and commanded that something should be given her to eat" (Mark 5:43). Since the critics were biased, the less they knew the better for all concerned.

The Delightful Deliverance . . . *Faith Triumphant*

"And he took the damsel by the hand, and said unto her, Talitha cumi, which is, being interpreted, Damsel, I say unto thee arise. And straightway the damsel arose, and walked; for she was of the age of twelve years. And they were astonished with a great aston- ishment. And he charged them straitly that no man should know it; and commanded that something should be given her to eat" (Mark 5:41–43).

Perhaps the father was unable to speak. His eyes were filled with tears. His arms were now around his restored child. Amazement was spreading among all who had witnessed the miracle. They were excited, and even the people in the street were astonished. The Preacher had done the impossible. "Talitha cumi" is Aramaic for "Maid, arise," and it seems strange to find this little bit of another language squeezed in among other words in the Gospel. Mark probably learned from Peter these unforgettable words as the Lord had spoken them, so Peter and Mark reproduced them. The parents were overjoyed. The others were excited, but, with care so charac- teristic of the Friend of children, Jesus remembered that little girls can be hungry! He commanded that she be given something to eat. Doubtless His command was obeyed, and when the parents saw their child happily eating what was provided, their cup was full and running over. Thus did the Lord reward a man, who, throwing aside his preconceived notions, desperately asked for help. "No good thing will he withhold from them that walk uprightly" (Ps. 84:11).

"Perhaps the Lord commanded the parents to refrain from broad- casting the news of the miracle because He knew His enemies would endeavor to make this event another cause for sarcastic com- ment. If they were capable of laughing when the parents were break- ing their hearts, they might also say the girl was never dead! The entire episode could become an object of ridicule as embittered men accused the parents of being sensationalists, fools, people who hast- ily jumped to conclusions. There are times when silence can be golden" (taken from the author's commentary, *Mark's Superb Gos- pel*, Kregel Publications, 1985, p. 147).

"And as he passed by, he saw Levi the son of Alphaeus sitting at the receipt of custom, and said unto him. Follow me. And he arose and followed him. And it came to pass, that, as Jesus sat at meat in his house, many publicans and sinners sat also together with Jesus and his disciples: for there were many, and they followed him. And when the scribes and Pharisees saw him eat with publicans and sinners, they said unto his disciples, How is it that he eateth and drinketh with publicans and sinners? When Jesus heard it, he saith unto them, They that are whole have no need of the physician, but they that are sick: I came not to call the righteous, but sinners to repentance."

Capernaum was one of the most important centers in Galilee, for through the city went caravans of many nations. There were numerous offices along the highways where imported goods were examined, assessed, and dues paid to government representatives. Matthew the son of Alphaeus was one of those men. The approach of Jesus to his table aroused considerable interest, for the Lord had no luggage to be examined and nothing to declare. With speculative eyes, Matthew looked at his client and then heard the words, "Follow me." There could not have been a more electrifying moment, for unlike Zacchaeus, Matthew knew the identity of Jesus. The inspired preaching of the Evangelist from Nazareth had stirred the city, and the cleansing of a leper had amazed the entire community. Every person talked about Jesus, and possibly Matthew had attended one of the meetings.

Much was at stake that day, for Matthew was an employee of the government and was accountable to an overseer. He was a man of the pen and was required to keep accurate records. Leaving his post in the middle of a busy day would cause problems—His records would be ruined, his employment lost, and his future threatened. As he continued to watch the Stranger with the fascinating smile and the laughing eyes, the Lord said to him, "Follow me." Suddenly the soul of the customs agent was deeply affected, and his obedience was instantaneous. Mark explained it was only the prelude to a banquet to which many publicans and sinners were invited. The Pharisees were outraged, but the Savior was aware of the consequences and decided to support His new friend.

If the host were asked why he had forsaken everything, he probably replied, "Look at Jesus." If people inquired about his plans for the future, he replied, "I want to stay with Him forever." Matthew transformed a home into a sanctuary. Once again the great Physician had made a house call. The details of that spontaneous response to the call of Christ are extremely fascinating.

A Glorious Celebration . . . *Expressing*

Matthew and Mark were content to write, "Jesus sat at meat in his house," but Luke, who was a medical doctor accustomed to keen observation, wrote, "And Levi made him a great feast in his own house" (Luke 5:29). That statement might be paraphrased, "And Levi supplied a magnificent banquet at his own expense." It was not an ordinary feast—it was a *great* feast that fully satisfied the needs of a multitude of guests. It commemorated the most wonderful moment in Matthew's life. The customs officer, unlike other disciples mentioned in the New Testament, was not the usual tax collector. He received custom fees obtained from travelers who brought goods from distant lands. That fact might explain why the critics directed their accusations against the guests; no one spoke ill of the host. The ordinary tax officials took money from reluctant taxpayers, but Matthew received the duties imposed upon business men who were able to recoup their losses from profits made in transactions. The merchants knew beforehand they would be required to pay import duty and could make the necessary adjustments in prices to reimburse themselves.

The feast had a dual purpose; it enabled Matthew to share his happiness with friends, but it was also a way by which he could express his love for the Savior. Unfortunately, there were many people who received much from the Lord but gave nothing in return (see Luke 17:12–19). A river without an outlet inevitably becomes a Dead Sea!

A Glad Confession . . . *Explaining*

The events of that memorable day were to be followed by widespread repercussions. The decision to follow Christ led to serious problems. Luke mentions the fact that having heard and accepted the invitation to follow Jesus, Matthew "left all, rose up, and followed him" (Luke 5:28). When the official closed his books and abandoned his lucrative occupation, his commitment to a new life was complete.

The rich young ruler considered discipleship to be too costly. He loved his possessions and refused to leave them. Matthew was different; he left everything except his pen! Hitherto he had written about money; henceforth he would describe miracles!

It seems significant that he never became famous for anything except his memoirs of the Lord. Simon Peter earned a reputation as a forceful speaker, John as a beloved pastor, Andrew as an earnest soul-winner, and Thomas as a man often filled with doubt. Matthew wrote a book that became immortal. He probably knew beforehand if any problems occurred at the feast, the Savior would help to solve them. When he worked together with the Lord they became a winning team. That delighted host was thrilled to see the Master enjoying His meal. Jesus had solved spiritual problems, and in return Matthew tried to show his gratitude. It was his way of saying, "Thank you, Lord, for saving my soul." Matthew had probably said to himself, "He did so much for me; what can I do for Him?" The subsequent banquet indicated the disciple was a cheerful giver and deserved the commendation of the Lord (see 2 Cor. 9:7).

A Gracious Companion . . . *Encouraging*

When the Lord and His new friend sat at the table, each was able to look at the other and exclaim, "He is mine!" The testimony of the disciple was enriched by the presence of the Lord, and the influence of the Master was increased by the radiant customs officer. Paul expressed the same truth when he wrote to the Corinthians saying, "For we are laborers together with God" (1 Cor. 3:9).

God often permits the future to be veiled in obscurity, yet Christians may be assured that His presence is abiding. When Paul was apprehended on the Damascus road, the Lord was there to deliver him. Many years later when the apostle was confronted by life threatening circumstances, the Lord again appeared to deliver His faithful servant (see Acts 22:17–18). During Paul's imprisonment "the Lord stood by him, and said, Be of good cheer, Paul, for as thou hast testified of me in Jerusalem, so must thou bear witness also at Rome" (see Acts 23:11). When Paul's ship was about to break into pieces, the apostle said, "For there stood by me this night the angel of God, whose I am, and whom I serve" (Acts 27:23). Throughout the long hazardous missionary journeys, the Savior revealed to His servant that he was indeed a laborer together *with God*; he was never alone.

Occasionally God's servants believe they have been forsaken and often become despondent. Elijah, who ran from Jezebel, exclaimed, "I have been very jealous for the Lord God of hosts: because the children of Israel have forsaken thy covenant, thrown down thine altars, and slain thy prophets with the sword; and I, even I only, am left; and they seek my life, to take it away" (1 Kings 19:14). The prophet was surprised when the Lord said, "Yet I have left me seven thousand in Israel, all the knees which have not bowed unto Baal, and every mouth which hath not kissed him" (1 Kings 19:18). God's servants should remember that although clouds may fill the sky, the sun never ceases to shine; every night is followed by a sunrise. Matthew enjoyed his banquet and was delighted to be able to minister to his Guest. After that day he developed into one of the unsung heroes of the Christian church.

A Great Continuance . . . *Endorsing*

Matthew did not claim to be the author of the gospel which bore his name. Paul, writing to the Christians in Rome, began by saying, "Paul, a servant of Jesus Christ, called to be an apostle, separated unto the gospel of God. . . . To all that be in Rome, beloved of God, called to be saints: Grace to you and peace from God our Father, and the Lord Jesus Christ" (Rom. 1:1, 7). This introduction was used in the letters sent to various churches and friends. The absence of any claim to authorship has often been used to assert the first gospel was not written by Matthew. This objection is hardly valid since the fathers of the early church stated categorically he was its author. Origen wrote, "The first gospel was written by Matthew, who was once a tax collector, but who was afterward an apostle of Jesus Christ, and it was prepared for the converts of Judaism, and published in the Hebrew tongue" (*Ecclestical History* 6.14.5). Irenaeus, Eusebius, Jerome, and Papias endorsed that conclusion (see *The Zondervan Pictorial Encyclopedia of the Bible*, vol. 4, pp. 122–123).

The absence of Matthew's claim to authorship might be indicative of his humility. He never sought the limelight of publicity, preferring a desk to a pulpit. He was the quiet apostle; he did not aspire to the first three—Peter, James, and John, who were present at the most important occasions in the Lord's ministry. Probably when the other disciples were preaching to crowds of people, Matthew remained at home writing his memoirs which became immortal. It appears evident that throughout his life the former customs agent remained true to his convictions and was a faithful servant of the Savior. When other professing Christians faltered and fell, he remained one of the most dependable of all the followers of Christ. When finally he stood once again in the presence of his Master, even the angels would have applauded when Christ said, "Well done, thou good and faithful servant: thou hast been faithful over a few things; I will make thee ruler over many things; enter thou into the joy of thy lord" (Matt. 25:21). This great author was never meant to be a profound preacher, but he did his utmost to extend the kingdom of Christ and left behind an example that every Christian should follow.

THE HOME OF SIMON PETER—
TO STIMULATE SERVICE (MARK 1:28–31)

The service in the synagogue had ended. The congregation was standing outside discussing the event that had electrified the sabbath audience. A demon possessed man had been miraculously delivered by Jesus of Nazareth, but the people could hardly believe what had happened. Peter was probably looking toward the shimmering waters of the Sea of Galilee, and perhaps the gentle breeze blowing upon the trees increased the music already within his soul. He saw the neighbors returning to their homes, but the Preacher remained motionless; none of the citizens had invited Him to dinner. The fisherman asked the Lord and His few disciples if they would like to come to his home to rest and meet his wife.

Many years later Mark wrote, "And forthwith, when they were come out of the synagogue, they entered into the house of Simon and Andrew, with James and John. But Simon's wife's mother lay sick of a fever, and anon they tell him of her. And he came and took her by the hand, and lifted her up; and immediately the fever left her and she ministered unto them" (Mark 1:29–31). Simon's wife had meals to prepare, a mother confined to her bed with a fever, and then she thought of the impending arrival of the additional guests. Had someone rebuked Peter, he would probably have shrugged his shoulders and replied, "She can manage it." Some wives placed in that position would have accused the husband of being thoughtless!

The hostess must have been very worried. Under normal circumstances she would have been assisted by her mother, but unfortunately the older woman was stricken with a great fever—she was burning up! When she heard of her son-in-law's action, she probably burned even more! Simon had been born without brains! Her daughter only had one pair of hands, and filled with frustration, the mother was helpless. Outside in the living room conversation might have been difficult. Then "anon they tell him of her." He smiled and rose to His feet. Jesus was not only a great Physician, He was exciting and gracious. His bedside manner was perfect. "And he came and took her by the hand and lifted her up, and immediately the fever left her, and she ministered unto them." Her instant recovery was astounding, but her response was even more amazing.

When Mark described the miracle, he never mentioned any returning of thanks. Apparently the mother did not even kneel at the

Lord's feet; she was urgently needed in the kitchen. If thanks were necessary, they could be given later. The Lord was hungry, the guests were waiting, her daughter was overworked. "Peter, get out of my way, I have a job to do." Within a short time the meal was served. She never received a doctor's bill. She knew a better way of paying her debt—she ministered to the Lord.

Perhaps within that home in Capernaum, Peter did most of the talking; the women did the work. Nothing more was recorded about that energetic mother-in-law, but it may be assumed her gratitude was overwhelming. The news of her healing spread swiftly through the city, and soon the house was surrounded by an immense crowd of neighbors who brought with them a variety of sick people. "And at even, when the sun did set, they brought unto him all that were diseased, and them that were possessed with devils. And all the city was gathered together at the door. And he healed many that were sick of diverse diseases, and cast out many devils; and suffered not the devils to speak, because they knew him" (Mark 1:32–34).

The streets were filled with many types of suffering people. The area resembled an overflow from a hospital. The sun was setting upon a scene never to be forgotten. When the Savior moved among the sufferers, His touch brought life and peace to their troubled souls. His ministry continued until, completely exhausted, the Lord sought refuge in the home of His friend. Maybe the grateful mother-in-law made His bed and gently closed the door, telling the others to lower their voices; the Master needed rest. "And in the morning, rising up a great while before day, he went out, and departed into a solitary place, and there prayed" (Mark 1:35).

Did the healed woman prepare a special breakfast and wonder why her Guest was not even in the house? She became a startling contrast to the citizens of Capernaum who, although they saw so much, deserved God's condemnation. It was not surprising when the Lord eventually said, "And thou, Capernaum, which art exalted unto heaven, shalt be cast down to hell: for if the mighty works, which have been done in thee, had been done in Sodom, it would have remained until this day" (Matt. 11:23). Nevertheless, in the midst of those unbelieving people lived the gracious woman who never forgot how the Lord had turned her night into day. It has often been claimed that Christians are saved to serve. This lady was a glorious example of that fact. The story suggests four things.

"But Simon's wife's mother lay sick of a fever." There were marshes in the area and high fevers were common. The name of Peter's wife was never mentioned, but we may assume that she and her husband provided a home for the mother-in-law. When Paul wrote to the Corinthians, he intimated that Simon Peter was a married man whose wife accompanied him on his missionary journeys (see 1 Cor. 9:5). According to the testimonies of two of the early church leaders, Clement of Alexandria and Eusebius, Peter's wife gave her life for the Lord, and her husband was compelled to watch as she was led away. His last words to her were, "Remember thou the Lord." That information provides a brief glimpse of the woman who welcomed the Lord and His disciples. She must have been very tolerant and patient; living with Simon Peter could not have been easy. It is not known how long her husband had been away from home, but it could not have been more than a few days. During his absence his mother-in-law had contracted this troublesome fever and was confined to her bed. If Peter knew what had taken place at home, he possibly was glad to escape responsibilities by attending the service in the local synagogue.

He never forgot that meeting in the sanctuary when his new Master addressed the congregation. During the sermon a raucous voice was heard interrupting the Speaker, and the disciple saw the man who was disturbing everybody. The demon possessed fellow was waving his arms and shouting, "Let us alone; what have we to do with thee, thou Jesus of Nazareth? art thou come to destroy us? I know thee who thou art, the Holy One of God" (Mark 1:24). The audience was perplexed, and some were afraid for the interrupter was known to be a dangerous man. Peter was amazed when Jesus said, "Hold thy peace, and come out of him." After the service he continued to think of these things, but trouble awaited him at home, and the miracle in the synagogue could not solve that problem.

Families can be like the Sea of Galilee. Some days they are covered by blue skies and attractive sunshine. At other times they are beset by storm clouds; the atmosphere is chilling, and the outlook bleak. Sickness brings its own problems, but when the illness is life threatening, increasing concern disturbs the entire household. The best thing to do with a problem is to lay it before Jesus. He can help when other sources fail.

129

It would have been interesting had the New Testament supplied more information concerning events on that memorable day. It is almost certain that Jesus was asked to visit Peter's home. It would have been surprising had He invited Himself. Simon was already a disciple, and since they were in the vicinity of his home, Peter said, "Master, would you like to come to my home to rest and meet my wife?" A fisherman's cottage was unpretentious, the furniture ordinary and unspectacular. If the wife were not given advance warning of the arrival of additional guests, she would have been agitated and worried as she endeavored to adjust to the new circumstances. Maybe she asked the guests to be seated in the living room while she hurried to the kitchen.

There is no mention of any conversation prior to the serving of the meal. Perhaps speaking was a little difficult as the men sat in the Lord's presence. Did Jesus ask about other members of the family, and was it then that "anon, they tell him of her"? (see Mark 1:30). Luke, who specialized in recording details, wrote, "And Simon's wife's mother was taken with a *great* fever; and they *besought* him for her" (Luke 4:38). The text suggests this was intercession and not a casual reference to the older woman. The statement is thought provoking, for evidently some person believed the Visitor was able to heal the mother. Was that informant influenced by the miraculous deliverance in the synagogue? Was that basically the reason why Simon invited Jesus to visit his home? It would be foolish to seek medicine when the great Physician was near. Many years after that event James wrote, "Ye have not, because ye ask not. Ye ask, and receive not, because ye ask amiss" (James 4:2–3).

The strength of the early church was its ability to pray. Those Christians spent more time on their knees than they did in pulpits. Prior to the Day of Pentecost, the saints prayed for ten days. Later, when Peter was brought out of the prison, he considered the nature of his miraculous deliverance and realized prayer was being made on his behalf. "And when he had considered the thing, he came to the house of Mary the mother of John, whose surname was Mark; where many were gathered together praying" (Acts 12:12). The Lord loved to share the problems of His followers, and that was evident during His visit to the home of Simon Peter.

"And he came and took her by the hand, and lifted her up, and immediately the fever left her" (Mark 1:31). *The Englishmen's Greek New Testament* says the mother-in-law was "oppressed with a great fever." *The New English Bible* translates the passage, "she was in the grip of a great fever." The woman was dangerously ill and helpless. It should be remembered that this miracle was performed early in the Lord's ministry. Later, when His power was known throughout the country, people were unimpressed, and some of His enemies attributed His success to His association with Beelzebub the prince of evil. The news regarding the mother of Simon's wife astonished the citizens of Capernaum, who hoped He would continue His efforts.

The woman was seriously ill when Jesus entered her bedroom. What she thought or said was never revealed, but the Lord graciously took her hand, rebuked the fever, and carefully helped her to sit up. *The New English Bible* translated the passage, "Her temperature returned to normal, and she got up and prepared a meal for them." During the time when Christ ministered, there were numerous magicians who claimed to be exorcists. The Talmud, which is the official collection of Jewish writings relative to Hebrew civil and religious laws, mentions the methods by which their performances were supposedly accomplished. An iron knife was tied by human hair to a thorn bush, certain Scriptures were read on successive days, and finally magical formulas were used to complete the procedure. Many people believed these deceivers to be indispensable. Peter met one of them in Samaria. "But there was a certain man, called Simon, which beforetime in the same city used sorcery, and bewitched the people of Samaria, giving out that himself was some great one: To whom they all gave heed, from the least to the greatest, saying, This man is the great power of God" (Acts 8:9–10). Paul also met similar men. "Then certain of the vagabond Jews, exorcists, took upon them to call over them which had evil spirits the name of the Lord Jesus, saying, We adjure you by Jesus whom Paul preacheth. And there were seven sons of one Sceva, a Jew, and chief of the priests, which did so. And the evil spirit answered and said, Jesus I know, and Paul I know; but who are ye? And the man in whom the evil spirit was leaped on them, and overcame them, and prevailed against them, so that they fled out of that house naked and wounded" (Acts 19:13–16).

131

These evil practitioners were completely different from the Savior who was not a deceiver. When He stood beside the bed of Peter's relative, His eyes were filled with compassion. Gently He touched her, and she was instantly healed. There was nothing ostentatious. What happened was dignified and inspiring. His touch brought peace to her soul.

The Stirring Praise . . . *Thrilling*

"And at even, when the sun did set, they brought unto him all that were diseased, and them that were possessed with devils. And all the city was gathered together at the door. And he healed many that were sick of diverse diseases, and cast out many devils; and suffered not the devils to speak because they knew him" (Mark 1:32–34). News travels fast! Dr. William Barkley, in his commentary on Mark states, "According to Jewish custom the main sabbath meal came immediately after the synagogue service, at the sixth hour, that is at twelve o'clock midday. The Jewish day began at 6 A.M. and the hours are counted from then." The healing of the mother-in-law probably occurred soon afterward. During the four or five hours that followed, the news of the miracle spread throughout Capernaum, and the people were filled with excitement. Families brought their sick, and the streets were filled with eager people. Mark said, "And all the city was gathered together at the door."

The air was filled with the joyful shouts of delivered people. Parents threw their arms around healed children, and others were amazed when demons were expelled. It was such an extraordinary scene that even angels might have watched in amazement. Somewhere in the background stood the mother whose deliverance caused the excitement. Maybe she wept for joy—who can tell? That wonderful woman never forgot the time when she first met the Savior. To her He would always be "The Great Physician."

THE HOME OF MARTHA, MARY, AND LAZARUS—
TO SHARE HIS SERENITY (LUKE 10:38)

It has often been claimed that comparisons are odious, and therefore it might be dangerous to compare homes mentioned in the New Testament. Houses are as different in design as people are in temperament. Nevertheless, it is probable that of all the dwellings in Palestine, Jesus preferred most the one owned by Martha, Mary, and Lazarus. It was like an oasis in what could easily have been a desert! As often as possible Jesus stayed with His friends. He was their favorite guest.

Certain details about that beloved family are extremely interesting. The Bible never mentions anything spoken by the only man in the house. Lazarus was a man of few words. Perhaps all the talking was done by his sisters! Nothing is said about him except that his illness terminated in death and resurrection, and that certain people feared his restoration to life would increase the popularity of the Savior. The story of his experiences remains unknown; his deeds were never recorded for posterity.

It seems strange that little is recorded of Mary's testimony except that she anointed the Lord with her very expensive ointment. Apparently she preferred to listen to Jesus rather than to spend time with other people. Two important things were said of her: (1) she sat at His feet (see Luke 10:39), and (2) she anointed the Lord with her ointment (see John 12:3). The Bethany family is mentioned three times in the Scriptures, and together the references provide an interesting study.

Fellowship Sought (Luke 10:38)

"Now it came to pass, as they went, that he entered into a certain village: and a certain woman named Martha received him into her house. And she had a sister called Mary, which also sat at Jesus' feet, and heard his word." It was Martha who first invited Jesus into her home; who complained, cleaned, and cooked. That delightful lady took her problem to Christ when, belatedly, He arrived after the death of Lazarus. Her residence was not a cathedral. It was probably only a cottage, but the Lord loved to go there. That fact should encourage and delight every Christian family. The Lord is able to transform a place of strain into a palace of serenity.

133

It would be interesting to know what happened before Martha invited Christ to supper. Had she attended any meeting or witnessed any miracle? Did she invite the Lord with the full approval of her family, or did she act alone believing her sister and brother would be pleased with her request? She approached the Lord and wistfully said, "Sir, would you be willing to come to my house to supper? My family would be delighted to welcome You and your friends." The Lord thanked her and gladly accepted the invitation. As a general rule, people are not invited into a home unless the host or hostess has a special reason for extending the invitation. Many Christians have speculated about Martha's request. Was she spiritually hungry, and did she believe the Savior could supply what she urgently needed?

When the Lord and the disciples arrived, they were given a great welcome, and He knew He had entered a haven of rest. Lazarus, the silent one, smiled; Mary listened; but Martha proceeded to prepare the evening meal. That was the commencement of a fellowship destined to charm the entire world. Probably Martha believed Jesus possessed something that she needed. His peace and joy superseded anything she had known. What He said was worth hearing; what He offered could not be obtained elsewhere. Martha quickly discovered that when Jesus entered her life and home, amazing things began to happen.

Perhaps she had listened to His teaching about the kingdom of God and, desiring to learn more, invited Him to supper. Maybe she did not realize His hand was knocking upon the door of her soul. This was one of the first indications that Jesus desired admittance to human hearts. When He sent a message to the church at Laodicea, He said, "Behold, I stand at the door and knock: if any man hear my voice, and open the door, I will come in to him, and will sup with him, and he with me" (Rev. 3:20). The home in Bethany was the only one to which Jesus went repeatedly. When He was about to be crucified, "he . . . went out of the city into Bethany; and he lodged there . . ." (Matt. 21:17). During moments of deep anguish the Lord found comfort among His dearest friends.

Martha welcomed the Lord and then went into the kitchen to prepare a meal. She was a magnificent hostess. Mary welcomed the Lord and then sat at His feet to listen. Let it be admitted that but for the industrious Martha the guests would have gone hungry.

Fellowship Spoiled (Luke 10:40–42)

"But Martha was cumbered about much serving, and came to him, and said, Lord, dost thou not care that my sister hath left me to serve alone? bid her therefore that she help me. And Jesus answered and said unto her, Martha, Martha, thou art careful and troubled about many things: But one thing is needful: and Mary hath chosen that good part, which shall not be taken away from her."

Poor Martha, she was all fingers and thumbs. Nothing was going right, and she was swiftly becoming an angry woman. The size of her kitchen remains unknown, but the nature of her complaint was obvious to everybody. At least sixteen people expected to be fed. If they were to sit or recline at a table, places had to be set with knives, forks, or whatever was used in those days, and plates put in order. Martha was trying to do six jobs at once, and—where was her sister? It is not difficult to understand her frustration as she looked in vain for the help urgently required. When she saw Mary sitting peacefully at the feet of the honored Guest, her soul exploded!

"Lord, dost thou not care . . ." It was unfortunate that she indirectly blamed the Lord for the disorder in the kitchen. Had she remained calm she might have said: "Master, I need a little help with the meal. Could you spare my sister for a few minutes, and then together we will be thrilled to listen." Martha was angry and frustrated; her thoughtless sister had no brains! Yet it was regrettable that she resented the attitude of the Lord. Devotion was admirable but not at another's expense. It was like giving a generous donation to a wonderful cause but using another person's money! The church has never ceased debating whether or not Martha's outburst was justified. It may be admitted that in a similar situation we might emulate her example.

Many years ago when I belonged to a traveling band of evangelists, we had a picnic lunch every day on the journey from one city to the next. We stopped along the highway and in the shade of a tree enjoyed what our cook provided. It was strange that after the meal some members of the party immediately developed an intense desire to enjoy their quiet time with the Lord. The washing of the dirty dishes was left to two of us, who postponed our prayer time until the utensils were cleaned and packed ready for the continuation of our journey. I confess with sincerity that occasionally I desired to use my tongue unlawfully! Maybe Martha would have understood and sympathized.

The Lord's reply to the irate woman was calm, considerate, and soothing, and it was significant that she never complained again. Probably Mary would have been useless in the kitchen, for her thoughts were with Jesus, and if she had not given attention to the kitchen chores, she might have become a nuisance. The inflammation within Martha's soul quickly subsided, and it was evident the great Physician had not lost His skill. The glorious fellowship of that evening could easily have been ruined. If an artist were commissioned to produce a portrait of Martha, he might paint a lady with her sleeves rolled up! If he were requested to do one of Mary, he would depict a woman with eyes shining like stars! It is strange and bewildering that members of a family can be so different. Some Christians love the Savior but are too busy to sit at His feet; others who live in conventions and special meetings are of no earthly use!

Fellowship Subdued (John 11:3–4)

It is refreshing to know that the disciples in Bethany were not angels. They were ordinary people who occasionally could be delightful, devoted, and disturbed by disappointment. Their eyes could fill with tears and their minds with distressing doubts. The illness and death of Lazarus were devastating, for it was difficult to believe their Friend, Jesus of Nazareth, could be insensitive to need. When He was informed of the critical illness of Lazarus, He did not respond and seemed unconcerned that the hearts of Mary and Martha were breaking. "When he had heard therefore that he was sick, he abode two days still in the same place where he was" (John 11:6).

Unless people have experienced similar periods of distress, it is impossible to understand the grief of those women. The Lord seemed to be unsympathetic during their time of need. Their request for help had been ignored, and it was extremely difficult to understand the apparent indifference of their Friend. When Martha went to meet Jesus, she said, "Lord, if thou hadst been here, my brother had not died. But I know, that even now, whatsoever thou wilt ask of God, God will give it thee" (John 11:21–22). The words even now shone as brilliant stars on a dark night and suggested the power of Christ was limitless. "Even now, when all other hope is dead, when nothing can be done to revive my brother's body, even now, You can do the impossible." She refused to abandon her quest, and relied implicitly upon His compassion. She remained baffled by His reluctance to respond to their earlier desire for assistance, and could not

136

understand His reasons for permitting them to suffer unprecedented anguish. Mary, who had sat at the Lord's feet, was now sitting alone at home, but Martha, who seldom sat still, was doing her utmost to solve problems.

She never forgot that meeting in the street, and remembered His words, "I am the resurrection, and the life: he that believeth in me, though he were dead, yet shall he live. And whosoever liveth and believeth in me shall never die. Believest thou this?" (John 11:25–26). Although both sisters misunderstood the Lord's motives and allowed sorrow to overshadow their faith, Christ never scolded them. He patiently led them into greater experiences of spiritual maturity. His success was evident when Martha exclaimed, "Yea Lord, I believe that thou art the Christ, the Son of God, which should come into the world" (John 11:27). Within the dark room of adversity she developed a clear picture of His majesty and immortality. This should be an encouragement to every Christian family. When the Savior is invited into a home, His help is assured in every emergency, and strain is replaced by serenity. When fever harasses the soul, the great Physician knows how to deal with the situation. Nevertheless, it is wise to remember that even He is hindered when closed doors prevent His entrance.

The apostle Paul referred to "the church in thine house" (Philem. 2). Christians first gathered in the home of John Mark and frequently in a part of the temple known as Solomon's Porch, but afterward they worshiped in homes where every meal became a love feast—where Christ was known in the breaking of the bread. When troubled people bowed in the Master's presence, frayed nerves were quieted and tempers disappeared. Each member of the congregation remembered that Jesus promised, "For where two or three are gathered together in my name, there am I in the midst of them" (Matt. 18:20). The Lord loved to make house calls, and although many years have passed since He ministered in Palestine, His desire has never changed.

Fellowship Shared (John 12:2)

The visits made by Jesus to the home in Bethany delighted the entire family. The fact that Mary sacrificed her valuable ointment and Martha prepared His meals indicated He was their favorite guest. He never imposed upon their kindness, and His arrival never caused concern to either of the women. Lazarus was always proud to sit with the Master to whom he owed his life. It could not have been easy to entertain thirteen men, but the Lord's presence was sufficient compensation even if they had been expected to entertain a multitude.

It was therefore with mixed feelings Martha and her sister heard their neighbor inviting them to supper. To grant his request would mean the loss of a night of fellowship, and although they had been included in the invitation, it would not be as intimate a gathering as they would have enjoyed in their own home. It may never be known whether or not they had regrets on that memorable evening. Perhaps, however, they were filled with delight, for they loved to share happiness with other people.

When the early Christians were oppressed by persecution, they went everywhere preaching the gospel. At that time mass media systems of communication were unknown, and yet before the end of the first century, the world had heard their message. That amazing result was achieved because the preachers were energized by an intense desire to share their faith. When the woman of Samaria met the Savior at Sychar's well, she was constrained to share her experience with neighbors, and her testimony led to a city-wide revival. The people afterward said, "Now we believe, not because of thy saying: for we have heard him ourselves, and know that this is indeed the Christ, the Savior of the world" (John 4:42). To share knowledge of the Lord is life's greatest privilege.

> The clock of life is wound but once;
> And no man has the power
> To tell just when the hands will stop,
> At late or early hour.
>
> To lose one's wealth is sad indeed,
> To lose one's health is more:
> To lose one's soul is such a loss:
> That no man can restore.

THE HOUSE OF THE PASSOVER—TO SUPPLY
A SEQUEL (LUKE 22:7–14)

"Then came the day of unleavened bread, when the passover must be killed. And he sent Peter and John, saying Go and prepare us the passover, that we may eat. And they said unto him, Where wilt thou that we prepare? And he said unto them, Behold, when ye are entered into the city, there shall a man meet you, bearing a pitcher of water; follow him into the house where he entereth in. And ye shall say unto the goodman of the house, The Master saith unto thee, Where is the guest chamber, where I shall eat the passover with my disciples? And he shall shew you a large upper room furnished; there make ready. And they went, and found as he had said unto them; and they made ready the passover. And when the hour was come, he sat down, and the twelve apostles with him."

This has always been one of the most intriguing stories of the New Testament. Throughout the history of the church scholars have debated concerning the identity of the man who owned the room in which Jesus and His followers celebrated the feast of Passover. Theologians believe he might have been the husband of Mary and the father of John Mark. Luke, who wrote the Acts of the Apostles, said that when Peter was miraculously released from prison, he eventually came to the house where *many* were gathered together praying (see Acts 12:12). Historians claim that three million people attended the feast, and accommodation for such a large number of pilgrims was difficult to find. That a large room was still available in Jerusalem supports the idea the Savior had already arranged with the owner for the special room to be reserved for His use. It was furnished and could easily have been rented. Evidently the disciples were unaware of any previous arrangements, for Peter and John were given specific instructions how to contact their guide. If the man were the father of John Mark, he could have been a committed believer. That he willingly cooperated with strangers suggests this was not his first contact with the Savior. Details of which nothing is known might have been previously planned.

Even if the man were the husband of Mary, he was not included among the apostles who sat at the table with the Lord. Probably the owner, whoever he might have been, celebrated the feast with his family in another part of the home. This story is one of the most fascinating accounts in the New Testament.

139

The Unusual Man . . . *Carrying Water*

Water carriers in the Middle East are always women. During visits to Jordan, Egypt, and Israel, I have never seen a man performing that task, but it is a common sight to see a woman balancing a waterpot on the top of her head or carrying a large jar on her shoulder as she either talks with friends or walks through a crowded street. The task is beneath the dignity of males. Bedouin women carry water over long distances to refresh their families. When Christ instructed His disciples to look for and follow *a man* carrying water, He either revealed arrangements had already been made or that He was omniscient and saw beforehand what would happen. Jesus knew the exact time of day when this event would take place. It is not known whether the man's wife was incapacitated, but evidently he was not concerned with the attitude of onlookers. If the Savior suggested this course of action, the fellow was very cooperative. If he had not received instructions, he was a most unusual man.

Dr. D. M. Spence, writing in the Pulpit Commentary, supplies interesting information. He says, "The name of the man who was to meet the disciples was omitted—purposely think Theophylac and others, lest the place of meeting should be prematurely known to Judas. 'Bearing a pitcher of water' would be an unusual sight in an Oriental city where the water is drawn by women. It is probable that the 'man' whom the Master foretold John and Peter would meet, was the master of the house, who according to Jewish custom, *on the 13th of Nisan, before the stars appeared in the heaven, had himself to go to the public fountain to draw the water with which the unleavened bread for the Passover was kneaded*" (quoted from *The Pulpit Commentary*, vol. 16, Luke, p. 196).

The Unselfish Man . . . *Surrendering His Premises*

"And he said unto them, Behold, when ye are entered into the city, there shall a man meet you, bearing a pitcher of water; *follow him into the house where he entereth in.* And ye shall say unto the goodman of the house, The Master saith unto thee, Where is the guestchamber, where I shall eat the passover with my disciples? And he shall shew you a large upper room furnished: there make ready."

Immense crowds from all over the world celebrated the feast of Passover. It was the busiest and most sacred time of Israel's year. Special legislation had to be passed by the rulers allowing visitors to erect tents on lawns or any piece of spare land. Formerly, pilgrims were required to camp within specified areas, but the multitudes made it necessary to erect tents wherever land could be found. People established temporary homes as far away as Bethany. A comparison might be made with the crowds of Moslems who annually visit their holy city of Mecca.

Jewish property owners joyfully anticipated every feast when they were able to augment their income. Even beggars in the street exploited the occasion. When many strangers sought accommodation, rents increased enormously, and property owners were able to ask any price desired. It was therefore obvious the friend who reserved his "large upper room" for Jesus could have rented his property for a large sum of money. Evidently, helping the Lord was more to be desired than increasing wealth.

When the disciples saw a man carrying a pitcher of water, they approached and repeated what their Master had commanded. Probably this was some kind of password pre-arranged by Jesus. The water carrier then led the way to the "goodman of the house" who was asked about the large upper room. This was a unique situation. Passover was the time for family celebrations, but on this occasion twelve men away from their homes were meeting with the Lord. It is extremely doubtful whether they understood the significance of the words spoken by Jesus, "With desire I have desired to eat *this passover* with you before I suffer." This was to be His final Passover. It would be a very special occasion.

The Unique Man . . . "*A Large Upper Room Furnished*"

Luke reminds us that the host had foreseen every need. The Lord and twelve disciples would be present, and whatever was considered necessary for their comfort was supplied by the owner of the premises. It is not known whether the men sat on the carpeted floor or reclined on couches. There would have been a table and perhaps benches. The kindly host had surveyed the room and decided nothing could be too good for the Master. Before the Passover began, that gracious host assured himself that Jesus would be pleased with everything arranged.

He was probably present when the disciples made preparations for the feast, but it would be interesting to know if he actually purchased the lamb used in the sacrificial ritual. Three million visitors were in Jerusalem, and each family needed a lamb. The demand on the sheep markets outside the city would have been phenomenal. Hebrew law insisted that each lamb be presented to the priests for examination, for animals with a blemish were never accepted for sacrifice. To meet the legal requirements of the occasion, crowds of people would be waiting in line to present their animals for inspection; delays were inevitable. Whether the disciples or the host purchased a lamb remains unimportant; *the animal never became a part of the Lord's Passover feast.*

When the certificate of authorization was obtained and taken back to the home, the owner was pleased. Everything was in readiness for the Master. "And when the hour was come, he [Jesus] sat down, and the twelve apostles with him" (Luke 22:14). What followed begs description. The herbs, spices and unleavened bread were all ready for use, but as the disciples remembered the usual procedure, they were mystified by the absence of meat. The lamb—even if it had been slain—was never used. Jesus took bread and wine and blessed the sacred symbols, but portions of the sacrifice were not distributed nor eaten. If anyone present asked, "Master, where is the lamb?" Jesus may have quietly replied, "I am the Lamb." "Whoso eateth my flesh, and drinketh my blood, hath eternal life, and I will raise him up at the last day. For my flesh is meat indeed, and my blood is drink indeed. He that eateth my flesh, and drinketh my blood, dwelleth in me, and I in him" (John 6:54–56). Did the disciples understand what was said? Maybe not then, but later the Holy Spirit enabled them to explain that truth, and it was said, "These that have turned the world upside down are come hither also" (Acts 17:6).

The presence of Christ transformed the upper room into a sanctuary, and when the Lord led His followers in the singing of a hymn, the music was destined to echo around the world. After the ascension of the Savior, the disciples returned "unto Jerusalem from the mount called Olivet, which is from Jerusalem a sabbath day's journey. And when they were come in, *they went up into an upper room*, where abode both Peter, and James, and John, and Andrew, Philip, and Thomas, Bartholomew, and Matthew, James the son of Alphaeus, and Simon Zelotes, and Judas the brother of James. These all continued with one accord in prayer and supplication, with the women, and Mary the mother of Jesus, and with his brethren" (Acts 1:12–14). The prayer meeting continued until the day of Pentecost when the Holy Spirit descended upon one hundred and twenty people—the place must have been *a large upper room*!

Later, it was written of Peter, "And when he had considered the thing [his miraculous escape from prison] he came to the house of Mary the mother of John, whose surname was Mark; *where many were gathered together praying.*" It is significant that *a large, upper room* was mentioned on several occasions; the place was well known and popular among early Christians. Was it the same room in which the Lord celebrated the Last Supper? When the Savior broke the bread and instituted a new feast, He began something to last throughout the church age. Prior to that final Passover, attention was directed toward a lamb; afterward everything was centered in the true Lamb of God who took away the sin of the world (see John 1:29).

The communion service meant everything to the early Christians. The room in which the Lord broke the bread was *large.* If it was the same place where 120 people were anointed by the Holy Spirit, then it was *very large.* Yet it should be remembered that Jesus said, "For where two or three are gathered together in my name, there am I in the midst of them" (Matt. 18:20). Had He said, "For where two or three hundred are met together in my name," He would have limited the areas in which His presence could be expected. The smaller number suggested that even the most humble dwelling can become a holy place. Perhaps in the final analysis it was providential that the name of the householder was never given. *Every* follower of Christ has the power to sanctify his own home and expect the great Physician to make frequent house calls.

The lights of Emmaus were clearly visible; the journey from Jerusalem was nearly terminated; yet Cleopas and his wife could not have cared less. Their hearts were singing. They could have walked with the Stranger forever! The previous week had been abnormally hectic. Their best Friend had been crucified, their hopes shattered, and their happiness destroyed.

The troubled man and woman would never forget the approach of the Stranger who thrilled their souls. Evidently He knew the Scriptures for "beginning at Moses and all the prophets, he expounded unto them in all the Scriptures the things concerning himself" (Luke 24:27). The sacred writings had become increasingly meaningful, and their problems had been solved. His sermon had been most inspiring, but unfortunately the delightful Traveler was about to leave. "And they drew nigh unto the village, whither they went, and he made as though he would have gone further. But they constrained him, saying, Abide with us: for it is toward evening, and the day is far spent. And he went in to tarry with them" (Luke 24:28–29). That couple was about to discover life is filled with surprises.

Those people had been amazed that their Companion knew so much about the prophetic writings. Was He a rabbi, a scholar, or a prophet? He quoted the Scriptures as if He had been their Author! They were beginning to believe dark clouds have a silver lining. What they considered to be a tragedy might be a unique triumph. The Stranger had explained how the death of Jesus was part of God's plan to bring redemption to the world and the Messiah to the throne of Israel. What He said was entrancing, and although He was evidently an important Person, He had entered their humble home. Although He knew they were unprepared for overnight guests, He calmly took a seat at their table. Everything about Him was astounding, and they were enthralled when He began to bless the food.

"And it came to pass, as he sat at meat with them, he took bread, and blessed it, and brake, and gave to them. And their eyes were opened, and they knew him; and he vanished out of their sight" (Luke 24:30–31). When they saw the nail prints in His hands, their depression vanished. "And they rose up the same hour, and returned to Jerusalem, and found the eleven gathered together, and them that were with them, Saying, The Lord is risen indeed, and hath appeared to Simon. And they told what things were done in the way, and how he was known of them in breaking of bread" (Luke 24:33–35). That delightful story contains five astonishing surprises.

The Strange Decision . . . *Charming*

Not much was recorded concerning these two lesser-known followers of Jesus. Some of the later church fathers believed that the wife of Cleopas watched as the Lord was crucified. Her husband remained unmentioned until he was returning to his home in Emmaus (see John 19:25). Apart from these references the existence of these people would have been unknown. On the other hand, some very important people were in Jerusalem, and upon them rested the future of the Christian church. They were puzzled and bewildered, for it was rumored their Master had risen from the dead, and Simon claimed he had been favored with a personal interview. Actually only a few miles separated the Emmaus travelers from their friends in Jerusalem, but in another sense, they were worlds apart. Nothing more was ever said concerning the couple from Emmaus, but the apostles were destined to become leaders of the Christian church. It seemed strange that the risen Lord should, more or less, bypass the important people in Jerusalem and go out of His way to intercept two travelers. Would it not have been more beneficial to instruct the apostles who would relay His message to the world?

It is encouraging to know God loves little people and is attentive to small matters. If He were only interested in millionaires, royalty, and folk with many talents, the majority of men and women would never enjoy His favor. Christ knew about a woman who touched the hem of His garment, about a child who was willing to sacrifice his lunch to help feed a multitude, and about a widow who placed two mites into the treasury. It was customary for the Creator of the world to help insignificant people in whom He delighted. That glorious fact is a source of unending encouragement. Most people may seem as helpless as babies, but adoring fathers, including the heavenly Father, love to hold little children in their arms.

Many questions concerning the resurrection of Christ remain unanswered. The Bible says that after He arose from the dead He stayed forty days with the disciples before He ascended into heaven. His body had been changed, for the mortal had put on immortality; yet to prove He was not a ghost, Jesus ate food before the disciples (see Luke 24:42–43). It would be interesting to know if, when, and where He slept during the five weeks prior to His ascension. During the period He appeared to His disciples but apart from those occasions, where did He spend His time, and where did He go? Amid all the questions that might be considered, one delightful detail becomes obvious. The two disciples who were returning to their home failed to recognize the Lord because Christ concealed His identity—He appeared in a disguise! Mark tells us that "After that, he appeared *in another form* unto two of them, as they walked, and went into the country. And they went and told it unto the residue: neither believed they them" (Mark 16:12–13). *The Living Bible* translates the text as follows: "Later that day, He appeared to two who were walking from Jerusalem into the country, but they didn't recognize him at first *because he had changed his appearance.*" The Savior was truly a *great* Physician; He desired to make His patients happy and *well.* Had He appeared in His usual manner, they would have recognized Him immediately, but the doubts, fears, and questions within their souls would have been untouched. He deliberately disguised Himself to deal with the unseen problems within their minds. Christians should expect their Master to be near even amid the mundane things of life. Rain is expected to fall from dark clouds. William Cowper wrote:

> Ye fearful saints, fresh courage take;
> The clouds ye so much dread:
> Are big with mercy, and will break
> In blessings on your head.

Paul enunciated a very important truth when he said to the Romans, "And we know that all things work together for good to them that love God, to them who are the called according to his purpose." When storms threaten the followers of Christ, they should expect Him to perform a miracle just as He did for the disciples on the Sea of Galilee. When "our eyes are holden" and we cannot recognize Him, we should never question His ability to save.

"Then he said unto them, O fools, and slow of heart to believe all that the prophets have spoken: Ought not Christ to have suffered these things, and to enter into his glory? And beginning at Moses and all the prophets, he expounded unto them in all the Scriptures the things concerning himself" (Luke 24:25–27). Probably the message delivered to the Emmaus travelers was the greatest sermon ever preached. It is known what Simon Peter and Stephen preached in the earliest days of the Christian church, but the subject matter used by the Savior remains a mystery. Perhaps God was content to mention only the source of the materials so that believers in every age would search and find for themselves the things to which He referred.

The first five books of the Bible are attributed to Moses, therefore his writings extended from the creation of man to the conquest of Canaan. The many prophets mentioned in the Scriptures covered the remaining period until the ministry of Malachi. It may be assumed that when the Lord instructed the two disciples, His data was drawn from the entire Old Testament, and He claimed to be the fulfillment of everything that had been predicted. It is impossible to avoid the conclusion that unless He was what He claimed to be, He was the most outrageous deceiver in history.

When the Lord spoke with Nicodemus, He mentioned that Moses had lifted up the serpent in the wilderness and suggested this related to His forthcoming crucifixion (see John 3:14–15). The prophet Isaiah described perfectly what was to happen hundreds of years later. What is now called the fifty-third chapter of his book supplied a vivid word picture of the death of the Son of God. Repeatedly throughout the Psalms, David mentioned details that were only fulfilled when Jesus of Nazareth died to reconcile sinners to God. The Almighty saw the end from the beginning and was able to paint on human canvas the scenes to be enacted when the Word was made flesh to dwell among us. The portrait of the Messiah was clearly stamped upon history, and when the risen Christ explained these facts to His fascinated listeners, their hearts burned within them. It should be emphasized that when the Lord spoke to His listeners, He spoke of things "concerning himself" (see Luke 24:27). Unless preachers center their messages in the Person of Christ, they are out of place in a pulpit! The world needs Jesus, but unfortunately modern soothsayers present orations that cannot heal broken hearts and homes. The words spoken by the ancient Greeks should be found in every pulpit, "Sir, we would see Jesus" (John 12:20–21).

The Startling Disappearance . . . *Compelling*

"And it came to pass, as he sat at meat with them, he took bread and blessed it, and brake, and gave to them. And their eyes were opened, and they knew him; and he vanished out of their sight. And they said one to another, Did not our heart burn within us, while he talked with us by the way, and while he opened to us the scriptures?" (Luke 24:30–32). It was unbelievable; one moment He was there, and the next He was gone! They looked at His empty chair and at each other, and then looked at the chair again. They were astonished and mystified. Suddenly both exclaimed, "He was the Lord." They were as people in a trance, hardly knowing what to do next. Readers may ask how that miraculous disappearance was accomplished, but the actions of God defy explanation. Luke in Acts 8:39 describes how, after the baptism of the Ethiopian eunuch, "the Spirit of the Lord caught away Philip, that the eunuch saw him no more. . . . But Philip was found in Azotus: and passing through he preached in all the cities, till he came to Caesarea."

The exact location of the oasis where the Ethiopian was baptized cannot be determined, but Ashdod or Azotus was at least twenty or thirty miles away. The Holy Spirit could have transported God's servant to the new location, and the same thing could have happened when Jesus left the home in Emmaus. Paul said, "For the Lord himself shall descend from heaven with a shout with the voice of the archangel, and with the trump of God: and the dead in Christ shall rise first: Then we which are alive and remain shall be caught up together with them in the clouds, to meet the Lord in the air: and so shall we ever be with the Lord" (1 Thess. 4:16–17). It would be most informative to discover the details associated with the removal of the Lord from Emmaus and the effect it had upon the couple left behind. They had been away for at least a week and would soon be retired for the night. Their friends in Jerusalem would also be preparing to sleep. Wisdom dictated that however important their message, it could wait until morning. Did the disciples consider these matters? Possibly they did, but the irresistible urge to reach their friends expelled any idea of delay. They had a story to tell, and the sooner they told it, the more pleased they would be. Blessed are the believers whose hearts are so filled with joy they cannot remain silent.

"And they rose up the same hour, and returned to Jerusalem, and found the eleven gathered together, and them that were with them, Saying, The Lord hath risen indeed, and hath appeared unto Simon. And they told what things were done in the way, and how he was known of them in breaking of bread" (Luke 24:33–35). A thrilling desire to tell others about the Lord is an excellent therapy for tired feet!

Several modern sites have been identified with Emmaus, but there is no conclusive evidence to prove which, if any, is authentic. The village would have been six or seven miles from Jerusalem, which necessitated a journey of one to two hours. The enthusiasm of the travelers might have shortened the time of travel, but in any case, their arrival in the city would have been late in the evening or in the early hours of the morning.

Mark said, "After that he appeared in another form unto two of them, as they walked, and went into the country. And they went and told it unto the residue: neither believed they them" (Mark 16:12–13). Luke endorsed that report when he wrote, "And they told what things were done in the way . . . Jesus himself stood in the midst of them, and saith unto them, Peace be unto you. But they were terrified and affrighted, and supposed that they had seen a spirit" (Luke 24:35–37). Probably the Lord returned along the same road to Jerusalem and arrived a few moments after His disciples. They were delivering their report when, "He stood in the midst of them . . ." No Christian witnesses alone. Standing in the shadows will be the Savior waiting to hear and endorse what is said about Him.

The church should be grateful to the disciples from Emmaus; had they remained in their village, their story might never have been told. Their obedience and testimony guaranteed an entrance into God's Hall of Fame.

SECTION THREE
The New Testament

"But Simon's wife's mother lay sick of a fever. . . . And he [Jesus] came and took her by the hand, and lifted her up; and immediately the fever left her, and she ministered unto them" (Mark 1:30–31).

One day when people traveled widely by stagecoach, a man went to purchase a ticket. He was asked if he wished to travel by first, second, or third class. He looked at the coach to ascertain that all the seats were identical and decided to travel third-class. As the coach rolled along the dusty road, he rejoiced over the way he had saved money. Other people who had paid more were no better off than he. As they approached a steep hill the horses decreased their speed, and the coach came to a halt. The driver jumped down from his seat, opened the door, and said, "First class passengers, keep your seats; second class passengers, get out and walk; third class passengers, get behind and push!"

There are many hills along the road of life, and the church needs members who will "get behind and push." Many people see the blue skies of promise and appreciate the scenery, but unfortunately they never use their muscles. They are content to let their fellow-passengers "get up, get out, and push!" Without the dedicated efforts of energetic Christians, the church "coach" would never move. It is interesting to consider the emphasis which the New Testament placed on the hands and arms of people healed by the Savior. If the eyes spoke of enlightenment and the feet as the means of walking with God, the hands suggested the service which might have been rendered to the Lord. Three notable examples invite investigation.

The Man Who Did Not Work (Luke 6:6)

"And it came to pass also on another sabbath, that he entered into the synagogue and taught: and there was a man whose right hand was withered." The author of the third Gospel was Luke, the beloved physician, and throughout his writings are evidences of authorship. As a doctor accustomed to making notes about his patients, he often included details which seemed insignificant. Here, he stated the man's problem was in his *right* hand. Webster's Dictionary describes palsy as "paralysis in any part of the body, sometimes accompanied by involuntary tremors . . . a shaking palsy, a chronic degenerative disease of the central nervous system characterized by tremors, muscular rigidity, weakness and a masklike expression." It is important to remember the afflicted man did not go to the synagogue to meet the Savior; he was already present when Jesus arrived. Probably he was known to most of the congregation. At first his uncontrollable movements and his twitching arms and legs disturbed the proceedings and annoyed the listeners. The Pharisees saw the fellow and wondered if he could be used in their efforts to humiliate the Lord. It is not known whether the afflicted man was cognizant of their scheme. His presence in the synagogue suggested three questions: (1) Was he there to worship Jehovah who apparently had permitted his misfortune? (2) Did he attend, hoping his affliction would arouse sympathy and produce charitable gifts? (3) Did the critics of Christ arrange his attendance so that he could be used in their questioning of Jesus?

It might be impossible to discern the true reason for the man's presence that day, but the Scriptures explain that his right hand was completely useless. He could see and understand, walk and approach the synagogue, sing and appreciate the psalms, but he was unable to use his right hand! He remained motionless while others did what needed to be done. It was an electrifying moment when Jesus said, "Stretch forth thine hand." Luke records "And he did so: and his hand was restored whole as the other" (Luke 6:10). The amazing miracle opened a door of unprecedented opportunity. Gratitude was expected, thanks were necessary, and service of varying kinds became possible. Unfortunately, none of these were mentioned by Luke. The man with the restored hand disappeared into oblivion. When in later days he used his hand, he served himself and not Christ. It was never recorded that he became a disciple of Jesus; he was content doing nothing! If he considered his attitude, he probably excused himself, not desiring to become involved in anything controversial. He would always be grateful to Jesus of Nazareth, but there were other men who were more capable in serving the itinerant Preacher. In one way or another he had paid for his transportation to heaven—let others get out and push!

The Mercenary Who Did Not Worship (Acts 3:2–8)

"And a certain man lame from his mother's womb was carried, whom they laid daily at the gate of the temple which is called Beautiful, to ask alms of them that entered into the temple; who seeing Peter and John about to go into the temple, asked an alms. . . . Then Peter said, Silver and gold have I none; but such as I have give I thee: In the name of Jesus Christ of Nazareth rise up and walk. And he took him by the right hand, and lifted him up: and immediately his feet and ankle bones received strength. And he leaping up stood, and walked, and entered with them into the temple, walking, and leaping, and praising God."

That beggar was probably one of the shrewdest men mentioned in the New Testament. His eyes were speculative, and he was a gifted actor. The place of his employment revealed he was a very astute operator. All beggars were not poor; some were wealthy because they appeared to be impoverished. To obtain a more intimate knowledge of the man who met Peter and John, it is necessary to consider certain facts. The beggar was over forty years of age (see Acts 4:22), and since even the children beg for money in the countries of the Middle East, this man had begged for the greater part of his life and was experienced in his profession. His facial expressions could influence even the most cynical observers. He could be pathetic or pleasant as occasion demanded.

The fellow could have solicited aid anywhere in Jerusalem, but he chose to operate at the gate of the temple. The reasons for his actions were obvious. Within the temple precincts were many attractions, and many of the visitors entered at the gate called Beautiful. Crowds of people were either entering or leaving, and the shrewd beggar realized worshipers would probably be generous. Every morning he arrived early, and he never departed until the gates closed. That was his daily occupation and counting money his greatest delight.

He seldom entered the temple, for that would have demanded time and a loss of an opportunity to solicit financial aid. From a distance he may have listened to the singing of the Levites, but their songs were never as attractive as the jingling of his coins. The lame man often saw the priests walking through the gate and possibly passed the time of day with them, but he seldom coveted their prayers. If he ever placed a coin in the treasury, he considered himself indispensable to the ongoing work of Jehovah. He was only interested in the end of services when, once again, possible donors would approach the gate. He had no desire to worship. He lived on the outside!

Then one day he saw two strangers approaching and instantly became alert. "Then Peter said, Silver and gold have I none; but such as I have give I thee: In the name of Jesus Christ of Nazareth rise up and walk. And he took him by the right hand, and lifted him up . . ." (Acts 3:6–7). That which followed almost defied description. New life flooded his body, and a strange power appeared to be operating upon his legs. Grasping the outstretched hand of his unknown Benefactor, the man rose to his feet and "entered with them, into the temple, walking, and leaping, and praising God." His life was completely transformed. There is no record that he ever appealed for alms again. His praises shattered the dignity of the sanctuary, and as astonished worshipers gathered around, the excited man continued his noisy outbursts. The following day when Peter and John were brought before the authorities, the beggar was with them (see Acts 4:14), but there, unfortunately, his story terminated. It would be illuminating to know what happened in the months that followed his remarkable recovery. Did he associate with the church and become one of the saints who went everywhere preaching the gospel? If that were true, Luke would have recorded those facts. His silence created doubts. Did the man spend his time in the sanctuary and forget other beggars who had been less fortunate? He resembled the man in the stagecoach. He was able and willing to walk, for he was with the apostles the day after the miracle. Yet there is no evidence that he joined other Christians in propelling the gospel chariot in its onward and uphill course. "Getting behind to push" was hard work, and he was unaccustomed to such labor.

My wife was very interested when a stranger said, "Mrs. Powell, your husband came to preach in my church. I had been a member there for many years. When the meetings terminated, I said to myself, 'I have been here for years, but there must be something more than I possess.' There was, and I found it. I am now an active member of The Gideons." His eyes reflected the warmth of his soul. He had become one of God's Third Class Passengers!

The Mother Who Did Not Wait (Mark 1:30–31)

"But Simon's wife's mother lay sick of a fever, and anon they tell him [Jesus] of her. And he came and took her by the hand, and lifted her up; and immediately the fever left her, and she ministered unto them."

It was the sabbath day in Capernaum and the people were leaving the synagogue. They had watched as Jesus of Nazareth expelled a demon from one of the congregation. Within sight of the Sea of Galilee they discussed what had been witnessed. Standing nearby was Simon, the son of Jonah (see Matt. 16:17), but his thoughts were occupied with a different matter. The time for the evening meal was approaching, and Jesus needed an invitation to dine. Perhaps Peter thought of his mother-in-law who was sick, but it seems probable he was more interested in what he could do for the Lord than in what Christ might do for him. Under ordinary circumstances no wife would be pleased to welcome five unexpected guests to dinner when her sick mother needed attention. To say the least, Simon was not famous for his consideration of others. He was a man motivated by impulses. He acted in haste and repented at leisure!

Simon's partner probably understood her husband and knew arguments and complaints would be useless. She asked them to be seated and arranged five extra places at the table. During the following moments someone thought of the mother in the bedroom, and "anon they tell him of her." Luke's account of this event is more informative. "And Simon's wife's mother was taken with a great fever; and they besought him for her. And he stood over her, and rebuked the fever; and it left her: and immediately she arose and ministered unto them" (Luke 4:38–39). *The Pulpit Commentary* on Mark says: "There were marshes in that district, hence the prevalence of fevers of a malignant character."

It is not difficult to imagine what that mother thought when she heard of the arrival of five guests and saw the worried look on the face of her daughter. Evidently someone within the home possessed faith, for it was written, "they besought him for her." The wisest way to handle any problem is to share it with Christ—He always knows what to do! When Jesus entered the bedroom to bring relief to the stricken lady, her soul was truly thrilled, but the resolution already forming within her mind was sensational. Her exit from the bedroom to the kitchen was accomplished in record time. If the members of her family advised caution and urged her to rest, she pushed them aside, saying, "Get out of my way. I have work to do . . . and immediately she arose and ministered unto them." Martha of Bethany would have admired her! Love is always expressed in faithful service. That woman's experiences might be summarized under four headings: (2) her difficulty; (2) her deliverance; (3) her determination; and (4) her delight. People who remain motionless when the Savior needs assistance are not true Christians. When that mother entered the kitchen she transformed the entire place. Not only her right hand, but every part of her body desired to serve her marvelous Benefactor. That wonderful mother-in-law worked so hard, that had she been in the stagecoach on the hill—even the horses might not have been necessary!

COME, GO, STAND, TASTE, BELIEVE

During my ministry in South Africa, I talked with a retired minister, and after discussing a very important question I said, "Well, maybe we shall have to leave this in God's hands." The old gentleman thought for a few seconds and then replied, "Maybe not. The Lord is very busy and has a lot to do." He appeared to be irreverent, but I now appreciate his point of view. We should never expect the Lord to do our work. There is a time in life when divine grace meets with human responsibility. That combination can perform miracles. Only when man has exhausted his resources can he justifiably expect the Lord to assume complete responsibility for what needs to be done. The ability of God never excuses human laziness. Perhaps Paul had that thought in mind when he urged his friends in Philippi to "work out their own salvation." They had an important part to play and were expected to cooperate with their Savior. There are five texts in the Bible which illustrate this great truth.

The Come and See of Conversion . . . *Sinners and Salvation* (John 1:39)

The Jordan Valley was filled with people who were relaxing between the exciting services held by John the Baptist. A meeting had just ended, but another would soon begin. Some families were enjoying a meal, others were relaxing, and many were speaking about the events which were taking place. Even the preacher was enjoying a respite as he conversed with two of his associates. "Again the next day after John stood, and two of his disciples; And looking upon Jesus as he walked, he saith, Behold the Lamb of God! And the two disciples heard him speak, and they followed Jesus. Then Jesus turned, and saw them following, and saith unto them, What seek ye? They said unto him, Rabbi . . . where dwellest thou? He saith unto them, Come and See. They came and saw where he dwelt, and abode with him that day; for it was about the tenth hour" (John 1:35–39).

It was never revealed where the Lord was staying. He could have been enjoying hospitality in a friend's home or living in a tent or cave. Wherever it was, the disciples were enthralled and were completely transformed by what they saw and heard. One whose name was Andrew could not rest until he shared his joy with his brother Simon. Christ knew the future of the church depended upon that memorable visit. Those men were destined to become valued disciples who would preach the gospel and change the world. Had they refused to accept His invitation to "Come and see," they might have remained ordinary people. It remains a mystery how an omnipotent God can be frustrated by the closed door of a human heart. He can and does seek admittance but never forces an entrance.

The Go and See of Concern . . . *Service and Sacrifice* (Mark 6:38)

The disciples were worried; their expressions revealed the unrest within their souls. They were frustrated and disliked the attitude of their Master. The day had seemed long and difficult. They were tired. It appeared to be providential when Jesus stepped into a boat to go to the other side of the lake. At least, so it appeared, they would be able to enjoy a few hours of relaxation. It was extremely annoying when the multitude ran around the northern part of the shore to await the arrival of the Savior. Frowns upon the faces of Simon Peter and his colleagues indicated displeasure, but when Jesus began another service, their spirits became disturbed. "And when the day was now far spent, his disciples came unto him, and said . . . Send them away, that they may go into the country round about, and into the villages, and buy themselves bread: for they have nothing to eat. He answered and said unto them, Give ye them to eat. And they say unto him, Shall we go and buy two hundred pennyworth of bread, and give them to eat? He saith unto them, How many loaves have ye? *Go and see*" (Mark 6:35–38). A similar incident is recorded in Mark 8:1–8, yet on both occasions, someone's cooperation enabled the Savior to feed a multitude of hungry people. A small boy who sacrificed his lunch enabled the Lord to supply a magnificent banquet.

Sometimes Christians are appalled by the immensity of their tasks when the achievement of their goals seems to be impossible. Despair should never replace determination, for when resources are minimal, no challenge is too difficult for the Savior to accept. He can feed multitudes, remove mountains, and walk on the water. Nevertheless, He used a boy's lunch, and on another occasion, Peter's boat.

The Stand and See of Confidence . . . *Stillness and Safety* (Exodus 14:13)

"And Moses said unto the people, Fear ye not, *stand* still, *and see* the salvation of the LORD, which he will shew you today: for the

Egyptians whom ye have seen today, ye shall see them again no more for ever." Confusion and fear had spread throughout Israel, for the Egyptian army was pursuing the helpless Hebrews. Defeat appeared to be inevitable. The anger of the nation became evident when some of the people said, "Because there were no graves in Egypt, hast thou taken us away to die in the wilderness? wherefore hast thou thus dealt with us, to carry us forth out of Egypt? Is not this the word that we did tell thee in Egypt, saying, Let us alone that we may serve the Egyptians? For it had been better for us to serve the Egyptians, than that we should die in the wilderness" (Ex. 14:11–12).

Their predicament seemed to be catastrophic. Enclosed by mountains and confronted by the sea they had no way by which to escape. The former captives feared they would be compelled to return to bondage. They did not possess weapons and had no military experience upon which to rely. Alone in magnificent grandeur, Moses remained unperturbed. His eyes shone as he raised his voice and said, "Fear ye not—Stand still and see—the salvation of the Lord." When the sea rolled back to provide a pathway to freedom, perhaps even the angels were elated. Then Moses and his people sang, "Thou didst blow with thy wind, the sea covered them: they sank as lead in the mighty waters. Who is like unto thee, O Lord among the gods? who is like thee, glorious in holiness, fearful in praises, doing wonders?" (Ex. 15:10–11).

The Lord knew how to protect His people, and it is refreshing to remember He has never lost that ability. There are occasions when He expects and demands our cooperation, but at others, the most effective way to help is to remain still. Each time God permits His people to be confronted by terrifying problems, He reveals His power to save. The Lord is never completely dependent upon us, for after all is said and done, He is still God!

The Taste and See of Content . . . *Satisfaction and Serenity* (Psalm 34:8)

David expressed his adoration when he wrote, "*O taste* and *see* that the LORD is good: blessed is the man that trusteth in him." He had been delivered from great danger, but the experience had been nerve-racking. Surrounded by treacherous enemies, David had taken advantage of the superstitions of the people and pretended to be insane. "And David . . . was sore afraid of Achish the king of Gath. And he changed his behavior before them, and feigned himself mad in their hands, and scrabbled on the doors of the gate, and let his spittle fall down upon his beard. Then said Achish unto his servants, Lo, ye see the man is mad: wherefore then have ye brought him to me? Have I need of mad men, that ye have brought this fellow to play the mad man in my presence? shall this fellow come into my house?" (1 Sam. 21:12–15).

There is no evidence that David had any experience as an actor, but his desperation spontaneously supplied that ability. His accusers believed insanity was the work of indwelling demons. They were afraid to execute their prisoner; the demons might be angry if their residence were destroyed. David was permitted to flee to the mountains where he reminisced and said, "This poor man cried, and the Lord heard him, and saved him out of all his troubles" (see the introduction to Ps. 34, and verse 6). He was overwhelmed and exultantly cried, "O taste and see that the Lord is good; blessed is the man who trusteth in him." Praise is the child of gratitude. Consideration of God's faithfulness always leads to thanksgiving.

The Believe and See of Conquest . . . *Sorrow and Survival* (John 11:40)

Martha and Mary were filled with sorrow; their brother had died. Their hearts and home were empty. The apparent indifference of their Friend, Jesus of Nazareth, had deepened their grief. Their future was bleak! Then they heard of the approach of the Lord. "Martha, as soon as she heard that Jesus was coming, went and met him" (John 11:20). Her meeting with the Lord produced results that echoed around the world. "Jesus said unto her: I am the resurrection, and the life: he that believeth in me, though he were dead, yet shall he live, And whosoever liveth and believeth in me, shall never die" (John 11:25–26). The words of the Savior became immortal. "Said I not unto thee, that, if thou wouldest *believe*, thou shouldest *see* the glory of God?" (John 11:40).

Faith laughs at impossibilities, but that is a lesson every Christian needs to learn. Circumstances can be threatening, but to stand with Christ in the midst of life's distress, to feel the pressure of His hand and hear His voice is the panacea for all ills.

The five steps to spiritual serenity are clearly defined. Come, go, stand, taste, and believe. They are sections of the highway that leads to the throne of grace.

THE UNSCALABLE MOUNTAINS OF GRACE (JOHN 7:46)

Some of the towering mountains of earth represent the most majestic objects of creation. A friend of mine in New Zealand described them as "decorations with which the Lord enhanced the beauty of earth."
Mount Everest and others of its type have been a challenge to intrepid climbers, and some people never rest until they have climbed to almost unreachable summits. I have seen men crawling like ants beneath protruding dangerous ledges, and have been amazed at the skill with which they drove stakes into the rocks to support them-selves as they endeavored to reach higher elevations. There are mountains of grace which glisten in eternal sunshine; their purity and splendor reflect the glory of God's heaven. To reach those lofty peaks may be very difficult, but it is possible to view the dazzling heights where Christ was quite "at home."

His Message Is Unsurpassable (John 7:45–46)

"Then came the officers to the chief priests and Pharisees; and they said unto them, Why have ye not brought him? The officers answered, Never man spake like this man." It was frustrating when the officials were helpless in the presence of the Man they were supposed to arrest. They had planned to end something considered to be nonsense. The Stranger from Galilee was disturbing the peace and could not be tolerated. Resolutely, the officials approached the meeting-place, but since there was no great urgency, they paused for a few moments to listen to the Speaker. That delay ruined their plans, for the Preacher was entrancingly interesting. The time passed quickly, and before they realized what was happening, the meeting ended. How could they arrest someone who had captivated them? That Man from Galilee had been amazingly eloquent. Later, when they returned to the Jewish leaders, they could only exclaim, "Never man spake like this man." They had seen and heard the Christ and would never forget the experience. Jesus had spoken with commanding authority, and even the scholarly people in the audience could not refute what had been said. When the Lord spoke about heaven, it was easy to believe He had been there; when He described the future, it appeared as if He had already seen it. Immense crowds were enthralled by His message, and His power to heal was unmistakable and irrefutable. Although the Savior never wrote a book, His words were destined to fill innumerable libraries. He never taught in a college or university, yet many who do reverently worship at His feet. His utterances constitute the greatest message ever given to mankind.

His Peace Is Unfathomable (Philippians 4:7)

"And the peace of God, which passeth all understanding, shall keep your hearts and minds through Christ Jesus." The Christians in Philippi were intimate friends of the apostle Paul, and they more than all others appreciated his words. He had been a prisoner in their jail. The church had been formed in tribulation, for when Paul and Silas first preached the gospel in the city, they were flogged and thrust into the innermost dungeon. Their songs at midnight electrified everybody and out of that emotional tempest came a peace beyond understanding. It was unnatural for men to sing the songs of Zion when their bodies were wracked with pain. It was unbelievable that suffering prisoners could be cheerful when their blood was falling upon the floor of the cell. Yet Luke described the scene by saying, "And at midnight Paul and Silas prayed, and sang praises unto God; and the prisoners heard them. And suddenly there was a great earthquake, so that the foundations of the prison were shaken: and immediately all the doors were opened, and every one's bands were loosed" (Acts 16:25–26).

When the evangelists heard the rumble of the earthquake and saw the doors swinging on their hinges, they probably smiled. Their God was still on the throne; their safety was assured. To describe that peace is sometimes difficult. Men in pain do not laugh. People enduring torture and death do not sing unless they are living above unpleasant circumstances. Then they resemble the ocean; the surface may be tempestuous, but in the depth of the sea calm remains undisturbed. Trusting saints know they are hidden with Christ in God and can say:

> Oh, the peace the Savior gives:
> Peace I never knew before;
> And the way has brighter grown
> Since I've learned to trust Him more.

It is worthy of attention that Paul began his epistles with the words, "Grace be unto you, *and peace*, from God our Father, and from the Lord Jesus Christ" (Phil. 1:2). The Lord was always the source of everything wonderful. The *peace of God* revealed a safe standing before the Lord. *Peace with God* indicated the tranquility of the soul indwelt by the Holy Spirit. That blessedness cannot easily be expressed in words. It is indefinable and almost inexpressible. It is the rare atmosphere that belongs to God's highest elevations.

His Joy Is Unspeakable (1 Peter 1:8)

The apostle Peter wrote to his friends saying, "Whom having not seen, ye love; in whom, though now ye see him not, yet believing, ye rejoice with joy unspeakable, and full of glory." It is significant that the readers of this letter could have found many reasons to complain. They were "strangers scattered throughout Pontus, Galatia, Cappadocia, Asia, and Bythinia" (1 Peter 1:1). James also sent a letter to the "twelve tribes which are scattered abroad" (James 1:1). That situation could have been related to the persecution that overwhelmed the early church. Luke wrote, "And at that time there was a great persecution against the church which was at Jerusalem; and they were all scattered abroad throughout the region of Judaea and Samaria" (Acts 8:1). For some unexplained reason the twelve apostles remained in Jerusalem, but the majority of the early Christians were forced to leave their homes and begin a new life in strange surroundings. It was truly significant that "they that were scattered abroad went every where preaching the word" (Acts 8:4). The Christians never complained about their misfortune. They turned scars into stars and, when they met strangers, made known the glorious news of Christ's death. Their happiness surpassed anything known by other people. Their joy was unspeakable and full of glory! Joy is the hallmark of the Christian, but as an old Scottish woman said, "It is better felt than telt!"

His Riches Are Unsearchable (Ephesians 3:8)

Paul said, "Unto me who am less than the least of all saints, is this grace given, that I should preach among the Gentiles the unsearchable riches of Christ." Perhaps the text is related to "the riches of his grace" mentioned in Ephesians 1:7. The apostle was an expert in the use of superlatives, and yet he realized the difficulty in trying to explain the abundance of wealth found in Christ. He was a man breathing fresh air, but there was always more oxygen in the atmosphere! He resembled a thirsty soul drinking water from a vast lake—his thirst was quenched but there remained enough refreshment to meet the need of the world. He was a prospector taking treasure from a vein of gold that ran through eternal hills. However much Paul discovered, it was nothing compared with the inexhaustible riches of the Prince of Glory.

God said, "For every beast of the forest is mine, and the cattle upon a thousand hills." That claim would be staggering to an ordinary person, and yet it was an understatement since Jehovah owns the universe. Every creature and gem belongs to God, for it was His ability that created the gold, diamonds, rubies, and everything else of value and placed them where men eventually discovered them. He made trees to grow, flowers to blossom, birds to sing, and rivers to flow. He produced color schemes and arranged that man should control everything that had been made. Hurricanes may be the breath of His anger, and earthquakes the shaking of His hand. "Who is like unto thee, O LORD, among the gods? who is like thee, glorious in holiness, fearful in praises, doing wonders?" (Ex. 15:11). Jehovah is almighty, and His riches are unsearchable. Humans have been privileged to discern a little of His wisdom and grace, but to know and understand everything about the Lord would be impossible.

His Love Is Unknowable (Ephesians 3:18–19)

Paul prayed for his friends in Ephesus requesting that they "May be able to comprehend with all saints what is the breadth, and length, and depth, and height; and to know the love of Christ, which passeth knowledge." It is not easy to know something that defies comprehension. Perhaps it is possible to know, in part, the mysteries of all these extraordinary texts, but to exhaust the wealth of the wisdom of God would be impossible. The poet was correct when he wrote:

> Could we with ink the ocean fill
> And were the skies of parchment made,
> Were every stalk on earth a quill
> And every man a scribe by trade,
> To write the love of God above
> Would drain the ocean dry,
> Nor could the scroll contain the whole
> Though stretched from sky to sky.

Man is only able to comprehend God as He reveals Himself. The writer to the Hebrews said, "God, who at sundry times and in diverse manners spake in times past unto the fathers by the prophets. Hath in these last days spoken unto us by his Son, whom he hath appointed heir of all things, by whom also he made the worlds" (Heb. 1:1–2). The most effective method by which one can understand the love of God is to become acquainted with the life of Christ. He touched lepers, welcomed small children to His arms, and claimed that God saw every injured sparrow falling to the ground. He fed hungry people, shared the grief of a widowed mother, and asked forgiveness for the enemies who crucified Him. Jesus saved a criminal who had nothing to give in return. John explained this when he wrote, "Herein is love, not that we loved God, but that he loved us, and sent his Son to be the propitiation for our sins" (1 John 4:10). Paul agreed with his colleague, for he wrote, "For scarcely for a righteous man will one die, yet peradventure for a good man some would even dare to die. But God commendeth his love toward us, in that, while we were yet sinners, Christ died for us" (Rom. 5:7–8). The Lord's words—love, peace, joy—and riches shone brilliantly against the background of human guilt. Together they resemble mountain peaks which reach the precincts of heaven. It is beyond comprehension that sinners are to be made like Him, but that indisputably is God's plan for His people. "We shall be like him" (1 John 3:2).

STEPHEN, THE GIANT AMONG
THE DWARFS (Acts 7:3, 8, 60)

An elderly Christian was asked what he desired most in life, and after a few moments reflection he replied, "I desire three things: (1) *To be found in Christ*; (2) *To be like Christ;* and (3) *To be with Christ.*" I have asked many people the same question. A little boy told me he wished to become a fireman. Students like books, misers covet money, politicians and athletes desire fame, alcoholics yearn for liquor and drugs. The testimony of the old Christian suggests sunshine on lofty mountain peaks overlooking valleys filled with fog. Stephen, the first Christian martyr, was a giant among dwarfs, a convert who matured quickly. Five thought-provoking details invite attention.

He Was Greatly Esteemed (Acts 6:5)

It may be safely assumed that Stephen was one of the first converts won by the early Christians. Probably he was attending the Feast of Pentecost when the apostles commenced preaching the gospel. He was never known as an associate of the original apostles and was not mentioned in any of the Gospels. It is therefore assumed he first believed in Christ when Peter delivered his testimony on the Day of Pentecost. Stephen was a Jew who had studied the Holy Writings, and when the claims of the Lord were presented, he realized that all for which he yearned could be found in Jesus of Nazareth. There were 3,000 converts in the initial meetings and 5,000 came later. Stephen became one of an army of 8,000 people, and it might have been easy for him to have been lost in the crowd. It was significant that within a short time he was well-known to an immense number of people. When the twelve apostles considered it necessary to appoint trustworthy persons to superintend the distribution of financial help to the impoverished widows within the church, the first person nominated was Stephen. Already he had gained the attention of the Christian leaders. How that happened so quickly may never be known, yet it is evident the young convert was recognized to be a man of outstanding ability who possessed qualities of leadership. *He was a man in Christ.* Stephen's earlier life remained undisclosed, but when he embraced the teachings of Christianity, he soon became a champion. Every day he became more like his Lord.

He Was Graciously Endowed (Acts 6:8)

"And Stephen, full of faith and power, did great wonders and miracles among the people." It appears incomprehensible that one so young in the faith should mature so quickly. Evidently success in Christian service is not entirely dependent upon academic distinction—valuable as that may be. Educational attainments can never be an effective substitute for the anointing of the Holy Spirit. As far as is known, Stephen was not a graduate of any theological institution and had not received a course in apologetics. His overwhelming success as a preacher of the gospel was the result of his being filled with the divine energy, which transformed an immature believer into a dynamic orator.

When confronted by disease, Stephen stretched forth his hand and healed the sick. He laughed at impossibilities. His exploits in the name of Christ electrified his audience. His fame spread far and wide, and at least to some degree, he became one of the most popular members of the early church. It might have been this phenomenon which brought him to the attention of the apostles who elected him to a place of importance within the organization of the expanding church. The man who was already *in Christ* was swiftly becoming *like Christ*.

He Was Genuinely Elected (Acts 6:3–5)

It is easily understood why the increasing needs of the church added to the pressure of administration. Converts were losing employment; widows were hungry. Many people who possessed property willingly sold their assets to contribute to the finances of the church. It quickly became evident that trustworthy officials were required to allocate funds to impoverished members. It was extremely complimentary when the entire church membership decided to recommend Stephen to superintend the allocation of church funds. Apparently he was the first choice made by the assembly. The people loved and admired him and considered him to be worthy of their trust. The Bible describes how the apostles refused to be burdened with mundane affairs, believing they should give all their attention to the study of God's Word and prayer. Their decision was accepted by their followers, but the man chosen to lead the selected committee was probably a more effective preacher than most of the men who refused to do his job. It was true that Simon Peter was the chief spokesman for the leaders of the church, that he was also the dynamic preacher used by God on the Day of Pentecost. Nevertheless, even his efforts did not surpass the thrilling address delivered by Stephen when he stood before his accusers. It was significant that when the Chief Administrator of the Kitchen preached before the Jewish Sanhedrin, God arranged that his astonishing sermon should be completely recorded for posterity. Fifty-two verses in the seventh chapter of the Acts of the Apostles are devoted entirely to the material used by Stephen in his outstanding oration. He began with Abraham and finished with Christ. It covered a period of 5,000 years and terminated with the most challenging appeal ever made by an evangelist. Evidently it was a spontaneous outpouring, and it would be interesting to know which listener ultimately wrote what was said. That such a preacher should be removed from the pulpit to become the administrator of widows' pensions seemed to be a travesty. Would he not have been more useful preaching to crowds in Jerusalem? Stephen never complained; he knew how to serve his Lord—anywhere.

He Was A Gifted Expositor (Acts 7:2–53)

The sermon revealed the type of life Stephen had enjoyed. No student could have memorized so much within a matter of days. That delightful man had always been a lover of the prophets and a student of their writings. Even had he been a regular worshiper at the synagogue, he could have expressed in minutes the entire course of Jewish history. Evidently this outstanding Christian had been "A Man of the Book." He was *faithful in his studies, fearless in his statements,* and *fervent in his spirit.*

It was significant that when he addressed the leaders of his nation his countenance resembled the face of an angel. It reflected the glow of the hidden fires which burned within his soul. Stephen knelt before the Lord before he appeared before people! His study had become an upper room. He feared God and no one else and provided an example for evangelists in every generation. All preachers should be students of the book! Unfortunately many ministers deviate from that path. They become involved with all types of social issues and work unceasingly with all kinds of organizations. Apparently, some of them have forgotten Paul's advice to Timothy, *"Preach the word"* (2 Tim. 4:2). When the cutting edge of a sword is ruined, it remains a piece of steel unfit to perform its vocation in battle. When a preacher ceases to be a prophet of God, he becomes

168

an ecclesiastical ornament within a religious building and cannot be that for which he was ordained. Even before Stephen recognized the wonder of his Savior, he was being prepared to become one of God's choicest servants.

He Was a Glorious Example (Acts 7:9–60)

The die was now cast; events were approaching their saddening climax. Accused, condemned, but undaunted, the young crusader had been taken to his place of execution. Angry men were lifting stones soon to become missiles. Perhaps there was increasing excitement in heaven, for the King of angels had risen from His place at the Father's right hand. A very special servant was about to come home, and angels had gathered to hail his arrival. "And they stoned Stephen, calling upon God and saying, Lord Jesus, receive my spirit. And he kneeled down, and cried with a loud voice, Lord, lay not this sin to their charge. And when he had said this, he fell asleep" (Acts 7:59–60).

The first Christian martyr was certainly *in Christ*. Indisputably, he was *like Christ*, for he asked forgiveness for his enemies (see Luke 23:34). It was a foregone conclusion that such a saint would ultimately be *with Christ*. When he awakened from his sleep, he was entranced to see the change in his surroundings. He was standing within the city of God and before him was the Savior with outstretched arms. This story reminds one of an old saint who, when he was about to leave this world, exclaimed, "If this is dying, it's wonderful."

"Nevertheless afterward" (Heb. 12:11).

Mrs. Charles Cowman, in her inspiring book *Streams in the Desert*, draws attention to a text in the epistle to the Hebrews and tells an interesting story about a man who owned a castle on the banks of the Rhine River in Germany. The innovative gentleman stretched wires between the towers of his elegant home, hoping the winds would play upon them and produce the music of an Aeolian harp. He waited for the breezes to blow but unfortunately was rewarded only by silence. Some time later a great storm devastated the area, and gale force winds blew upon the castle. When the gentleman stood at a window to survey the countryside, he heard the most entrancing sounds, for the hurricane was playing upon his wires, and the music could be heard even above the noise of the storm. Mrs. Cowman quoted a delightful poem:

> Rain, rain,
> Beating against the pane:
> How endlessly it pours
> Out of doors,
> From the blackened sky;
> Wonder why?
>
> Flowers, flowers,
> Upspringing after showers,
> Blossoming fresh and fair,
> Everywhere!
> Ah, God has explained
> Why it rained.

There is nothing more entrancing than a bright spring morning which follows a tempestuous night. The Bible supplies thrilling examples of this fact.

Job . . . *The Glowing Heart* (Job 23:10)

The story of the sufferings of Job presents difficulties. To say the least, it seemed unfair that a righteous man should be compelled to suffer. The Bible explains how the event was permitted by Jehovah, but the fact remains that for the harassed farmer, it was hard to understand why God allowed such devastating experiences to overwhelm a good man. If Job ever asked, "Why has this happened to me?" he expressed the thoughts of innumerable people. The compensation given later by the Almighty was too late to ease the pain caused by the initial tragedies.

"Nevertheless afterward" when the patriarch reminisced, he discovered his gains exceeded his losses. It is believed Job was one of the earliest humans, and the book which bears his name was the first volume known to mankind. His limitless patience set an example for all descendants to follow, but among the somber colors and designs of his tragic experience was a golden thread which made everything worthwhile. The troubled man learned his greatest lesson during the stormiest period of his life.

There came a time when Job envied people who had died. As he looked through tear-filled eyes, it appeared as if deceased neighbors were extremely fortunate. Their sorrows had been buried; their sufferings ceased when death terminated pain. They had been released from discomfort and anguish, and although the people were dead, never again would they encounter the problems which had beset them during their lifetime. Desperately, Job said, "Why died I not from the womb? . . . for now should I have lain still and been quiet, I should have slept; then had I been at rest. . . . There the wicked cease from troubling; and there the weary be at rest" (Job 3:11–17). I am reminded of a lady who said, "I am dying and have no hope for the future. I believe death terminates everything. I have made my last will and testament and arranged that my body be cremated and its ashes scattered over the sea." That despondent woman believed she was about to enter into an unconsciousness from which she would never emerge. Job could have sympathized with her.

It is not known how he graduated from his fatalism. Somewhere amid the depressing events of his life, a new idea began to change his outlook, and he was no longer convinced death was the end of existence. Perhaps it seemed incongruous that God should have nothing better to offer than eternal oblivion. Whether or not he shared his ideas with friends has not been revealed, but there came a day when the patriarch said, "If a man die, shall he live again?" (Job 14:14). That statement represented a small light in the blackness which had surrounded his soul. He was no longer sure his earlier belief was valid. Could it be possible that beyond time's horizon lay another world—a place of immortality? Probably Job remained unaware that God was beginning to reward his loyalty. His God was the Jehovah of the present; but could He also be the Lord of the future? Perhaps, after all, there was hope of eternal life!

When he advanced along his path of discovery, things happened quickly, and finally, doubts were overcome and questions answered. Exultantly he exclaimed, "For I know that my redeemer liveth, and that he shall stand at the latter day upon the earth: And though after my skin worms destroy this body, yet in my flesh shall I see God; Whom I shall see for myself, and mine eyes shall behold, and not another" (Job 19:25–27). That thrilling revelation completely changed Job's outlook. He could have said with Paul, "For I reckon that the sufferings of this present time are not worthy to be compared with the glory which shall be revealed in us" (Rom. 8:18).

As the clouds parted and the sun began to shine upon the patriarch, his blessings were unprecedented. He remembered the dark valley through which he had traveled, but of greater importance was the new understanding gained in transit. The grave, which only offered oblivion, had become an entrance into everlasting bliss. His Redeemer intended to descend to earth, and Job would meet Him face to face! He smiled. His ordeal was over. He had discovered something in his valley of darkness that might have remained unknown had his prosperity been uninterrupted.

The Hebrew Young Men . . . *The Gracious Helper* (Daniel 3:25)

Their outlook was bleak. It was difficult not to be frightened. Nebuchadnezzar, the king of Babylon, was exceedingly angry. His ego had been offended, and he was determined the arrogant Hebrews would pay for their indiscretions. Had the monarch been less opinionated, he would have recognized the animosity of his counselors. They detested Daniel who had been elevated to a position of importance within the kingdom, and consequently, they also despised his friends. Three young men had been made rulers within the province of Babylon, and the noblemen were envious. "Wherefore at that time certain Chaldeans came near, and accused the Jews They spake and said to the king. There are certain Jews whom thou hast set over the affairs of the province of Babylon, Shadrach, Meshach, and Abednego; these men, O king, have not regarded thee: they serve not thy gods, nor worship the golden image which thou hast set up. Then Nebuchadnezzar in his rage and fury commanded to bring Shadrach, Meshach, and Abednego" (Dan. 3:8–13).

172

When the Hebrews reiterated their refusal to bow before an image, the monarch was incensed and "commanded the most mighty men that were in his army to bind Shadrach, Meshach, and Abednego, and to cast them into the burning fiery furnace" (Dan. 3:20). Those moments were terrifying, but the prisoners believed it was better to die honorably than to live in shame.

To a degree their spiritual development resembled that of Job. At first they knew little if anything of spiritual realities. They had been born in captivity, and any knowledge of God had been gleaned from the teaching of the elders. The fathers of the nation were determined to preserve their faith, and alongside the rivers of Babylon they instructed the children. There the boys learned about Jehovah and His chosen people. It became evident that their lessons made an impact upon the scholars, for when they were commanded to eat prohibited food, their refusal made the prince of the eunuchs say, "I fear my lord the king, who hath appointed your meat, and your drink: for why should he see your faces worse liking than the children which are of your sort? Then shall ye make me endanger my head to the king" (Dan. 1:10). There is no evidence that Daniel's companions had any personal relationship with Jehovah. They believed what they had been taught and refused to violate the commandments of their fathers' God.

At a later date their faith led to a tremendous experience. The irritable monarch could not remember a dream that had disturbed his slumber. When he sought aid from his astrologers and wise men, they were unable to satisfy his demands, and in his rage Nebuchadnezzar threatened to slay them. "Then Daniel went to his house, and made the thing known to Hananiah, Mishael, and Azariah, his companions: That they should desire mercies of the God of heaven concerning this secret, that Daniel and his fellows should not perish with the rest of the wise men of Babylon" (Dan. 2:17–18). Apparently this was the first time these young men were asked to pray. They believed in the God who had helped Israel in past years, but now they were to discover Jehovah could repeat His earlier actions. Their spiritual education was not yet complete. When they were about to be cast into the furnace, they needed a Savior who could deliver them from imminent peril. Could there be such a God? They were resolute in their decision. If He could help them they would love Him forever; but if not, they would still obey His commands.

Their ordeal was over—or was it? They were dropping into the flames. There was no turning back. "Then Nebuchadnezzar the king was astonied, and rose up in haste, and spake, and said unto his counselors, Did not we cast three men bound into the midst of the fire? They answered and said unto the king, True, O king. He answered and said, Lo, I see four men loose, walking in the midst of the fire, and they have no hurt; and the form of the fourth is like the Son of God" (Dan. 3:24–25). That story explains how God became a reality to people who trusted Him.

"Nevertheless afterward" there were moments when they relived their experience and were elated as they remembered their spiritual growth. The God of the past was also the Lord of the present. Jehovah, who resided in heaven, could also come to earth to be with His servants. Evidently He could have prevented their being thrown into the flames, but that would have been a mistake. The devouring fire was a school-house in which life's important lessons were taught. The ordeal not only destroyed their bonds, it opened their eyes to recognize the sovereignty of God. Those Hebrews had contemplated the future and wondered; they remembered the past and worshiped.

Paul . . . *The Guiding Hand* (Acts 27:23–24)

The waves were devastating, the storm unrelenting. Even the captain of the ship had lost hope of surviving the onslaught of the sea. His ship was being driven to destruction. Years later, when Luke wrote his memoirs of that terrible occasion, he said, "There arose against it a tempestuous wind, called Euroclydon. And when the ship was caught, and could not bear up into the wind, we let her drive. And running under a certain island which is called Clauda, we had much work to come by the boat. . . . And we being exceedingly tossed with a tempest, the next day they lightened the ship; And the third day we cast out with our own hands the tackling of the ship. And when neither sun nor stars in many days appeared, and no small tempest lay on us, all hope that we should be saved was then taken away" (Acts 27:14–20).

To be adrift in such a vast expanse of raging waters was an experience never to be forgotten. Only one man on that foundering vessel knew God continued to control the elements. "The Mediterranean Sea is the largest enclosed sea in the world, and is connected with the open sea only by the narrow strait of Gibraltar. Its area is

174

estimated at 965,000 square miles. The island of Malta, the largest of the islands, covers an area of only 95 square miles" (quoted from *Funk and Wagnalls Encyclopedia*, vol. 16, pp. 5790, 5948). No person aboard that ship knew the location of the vessel, and since it was completely out of control, the crew and passengers could only hope and pray for a miracle.

It is now recognized that throughout the duration of that voyage, God controlled the weather. He did not need stars nor navigational instruments; sails and tillers were not required. The currents in the ocean took the ship unerringly to the place where Paul was needed. The vessel could not sink until God permitted it so to do. Even the gale was subject to the divine will. The people who lived on the island of Malta needed to hear the Gospel, and the father of the governor was seriously ill. If the storm had not *driven* Paul's ship, the preacher would have arrived too late to save that man's life. Unerringly, through days and nights of unprecedented anguish, God piloted the vessel, and when the episode ended, Paul and his companions were able to reminisce and know that the Lord had ordained every detail of their harrowing experience. Once again the words, "Nevertheless afterward" became attractive! It has often been claimed that hindsight is better than foresight, but the accuracy of the statement may be challenged. Looking back at threatening storms cannot supply the strength needed to endure. Retrospect can only promote understanding. Paul with unerring foresight saw what God intended to do and was able to say, "For there stood by me this night the angel of God, whose I am, and whom I serve, Saying, Fear not, Paul; thou must be brought before Caesar: and, lo, God hath given thee all them that sail with thee. Wherefore, sirs, be of good cheer: for I believe God, that it shall be even as it was told me" (Acts 27:23–25).

> 'Tis far far better to let Him choose
> The way that we should take:
> If only we leave our lives to Him,
> He will guide without mistake.
> We in our blindness would never choose
> A pathway dark and rough:
> And so we should ever find in Him
> The God Who is enough!

Author Unknown

GOD'S GREATEST PROVISION, MAN'S MOST EFFECTIVE PLEA—"THE PRECIOUS BLOOD OF CHRIST" (1 PETER 1:19)

Dr. Berry, one of the most famous of British preachers, was asked by a young woman to get her mother into the kingdom of God before it was too late! That scholarly minister described later how he sat beside the dying lady and gave extracts from some of his most acclaimed sermons. She responded saying, "No, not that! Get me in." Then he repeated what he had heard when he was only a small child. He said, "Mother, there is a great God in heaven who loves us . . ." "Ah," she exclaimed, "that's better." The preacher continued. "Yes, He sent His Son, the Lord Jesus, down to earth, and because He died for you and me, His precious blood can make us clean." Suddenly, she replied, "Of course, that's it. His blood can make us clean." Later, when he told his story, Dr. Berry exultantly exclaimed, "I got her in; I got her in. And then, I slipped in myself."

Through His Blood . . . *Pardon is Received* (Ephesians 1:7)

Paul wrote to the Christians in Ephesus saying, "In whom [Christ] we have redemption through his blood, the forgiveness of sins, according to the riches of his grace." That was the basic principle of the message the apostle preached throughout his ministry. Redemption was typified and portrayed by the Jewish Passover, practiced throughout Hebrew history, and proclaimed by every New Testament evangelist. The Passover Feast continued to be a reminder of the night when the first born of every Egyptian family died. Yet the astonishing fact remained that although the captives were probably equally as sinful, their first born were spared, not because they had a prior claim on the kindness of Jehovah but by the fact they were protected by the blood of a slain lamb. Responding to the instruction of Moses, the Israelites obeyed the commandments of God, placed the evidence of sacrifice on their homes, and confidently closed the doors, knowing God would honor His promise.

Throughout the following centuries all Hebrew parents explained to their children the significance of the Passover, and the feast became the most solemn event in the calendar. Even the boys and girls knew the nation existed, not because of the importance of their lineage, but because their forefathers had believed God. Thus in a strange but entrancing manner, the Lord prepared the nation for the

176

time when John the Baptist would proclaim, "Behold the Lamb of God which taketh away the sin of the world" (John 1:29). The scope and magnificence of Christ's sacrifice was indicated in the fact that unlike the Passover lamb which availed only for a limited number of people, the atoning death of the Savior gave hope to people of all nations in every generation. Yet its effectiveness could never be realized until faith and obedience to God made that possible. Happy are they who can say:

> I have no other argument
> I need no other plea:
> It is enough that Jesus died,
> And that He died for me.

Through His Blood . . . *Peace is Realized* (Colossians 1:20)

Peace is the assurance within the human heart that a state of war has ended. Writing to the Colossians, Paul said, "And, having made peace through the blood of his cross, by him to reconcile all things unto himself." The difficulties which existed between God and man were resolved through the death of the Savior. When Jesus cried, "It is finished," He knew that what He was commissioned to do had been successfully accomplished. The preachers within the early church endorsed that message when they proclaimed that faith in the Redeemer brought the peace of God to the troubled souls of men and women. Paul wrote to the Christians in Rome, saying, "Therefore being justified by faith, we have peace with God" (Rom. 5:1). This was emphasized when the writer to the Hebrews said, "For if the blood of bulls and of goats, and the ashes of an heifer sprinkling the unclean, sanctifieth to the purifying of the flesh: How much more shall the blood of Christ, who through the eternal Spirit offered himself without spot to God, purge your conscience from dead works to serve the living God?" (Heb. 9:13–14).

A disturbed conscience is not a comforting companion. The memory of moral decadence and repeated failure to achieve spiritual ambitions destroys the tranquility of the human spirit. Guilt is a burden too heavy to be carried. Yet the serenity of the soul can be restored when forgiveness thrills the recipient. God said, "Come now, and let us reason together, saith the LORD. Though your sins be as scarlet, they shall be as white as snow; though they be red like crimson, they shall be as wool" (Isa. 1:18). The Savior said, "Verily, verily, I say unto you, he that heareth my word, and believeth on him that sent me, hath everlasting life, and shall not come into condemnation; but is passed from death unto life" (John 5:24). This glorious promise endorses the words spoken through the prophet, "I will forgive their iniquity, and I will remember their sin no more" (Jer. 31:34). Men and women can know they have been reconciled to God—that their feud with the Almighty has terminated.

Through His Blood . . . *Power is Released* (Revelation 12:10–11)

"And I heard a loud voice saying in heaven, Now is come salvation, and strength, and the kingdom of our God, and the power of Christ: for the accuser of our brethren is cast down, which accused them before our God day and night. And they overcame him by the blood of the Lamb, and by the word of their testimony; and they loved not their lives unto the death."

To be acquainted with the power of Christ's redeeming blood is probably the greatest acquisition of any Christian. It is the invisible shield that protects beleaguered souls from satanic domination. When a believer claims that protective power, the forces of evil become inoperative. Conflicts are often lost because men and women rely upon human sufficiency, and their resources are never adequate. The apostle John expressed the most valuable of all doctrines when he explained how Satan was overcome when the saints exercised their God-given authority and used against the enemy their strongest weapon—*the blood of the Lamb.*

I shall never forget a night when an evangelistic service was threatened by a very emotional woman. The unfortunate woman had lost control of her feelings, and her screams and shouts disturbed the entire congregation. When she howled like a wolf, I sat with the pastor and feared the meeting would be ruined. Evidently this was a direct effort by Satan to prevent the preaching of the gospel. Desperately I began to pray. I said, "Lord, I cannot manage this situation, but I plead the protective power of Thy precious blood. Please Lord, cover this meeting and prevent the evil one from interfering." Within a few moments the woman became silent and remained motionless throughout the remaining part of the service. Afterward the pastor said, "I saw your lips moving." I replied, "I was asking the Lord to protect the service with the power of His precious blood." It seems evident that spiritual battles are often lost because Christians fail to use the weapons God has made available.

Through His Blood . . . *Purity is Restored* (1 John 1:7)

"But if we walk in the light, as he is in the light, we have fellowship one with another, and the blood of Jesus Christ his Son cleanseth us from all sin." This was among the greatest of John's statements. The apostle spoke of continuous cleansing. This was not only a purification of the soul, but also a maintenance of that condition. Nevertheless, John was careful to emphasize this blessing was conditional. He said, "*If* we walk in the light . . ." God's abundant grace is not a license to sin. People who walk in the light yield to the divine will. Deliberate sinning is prohibited, moral pitfalls avoided, and everything contrary to the directions of the Holy Spirit outlawed. There are sins of which some Christians may be unaware—sins of omission. As a Christian grows in grace, he learns that certain things thought to be harmless might become dangerous. Therefore, in cooperation with the Lord, he rejects and avoids them. This is walking in the light, the secret of enjoying fellowship with the Lord. Christians filled with the Holy Spirit never do anything that is obnoxious. The Lord said, "If ye love me, keep my commandments." When people persistently resist the suggestions of the Divine Spirit, they are not walking in the light and are not continually cleansed from their sins. Their conscience becomes a source of annoyance, usefulness in Christ's service is impaired, and, as was the case with David, the joy of salvation is lost (Ps. 51:11–12).

Unfortunately, many Christians who have willfully transgressed have fallen into error believing they have committed an unpardonable sin. They believe it is impossible to restore former relationships with God. The future is therefore ruined, and the rest of their life is disastrous. Continuing frustration and defeat lead to tragedy. Dismay and shame produce frightening results. It then becomes easy for people to believe it is better to die than to live in misery. That conclusion is often the forerunner of suicide, when everything of value is destroyed. It should be remembered that the most important work of the Holy Spirit is the presentation of the Savior. Jesus said, "Howbeit when he, the Spirit of truth, is come, he will guide you into all truth: for he shall not speak of himself; but whatsoever he shall hear, that shall he speak: and he will shew you things to come. He shall glorify me: for he shall receive of mine, and shall shew it unto you" (John 16:13–14). The sin against the Holy Spirit is the rejection of His message—the failure to accept the Lord whom He presents. There is no forgiveness for that sin, either on earth or in eternity.

It is difficult to believe that anyone who truly loved Christ could curse Him. Saints make mistakes, but they would never renounce their Lord. Simon Peter disappointed his Master but wept his way back to the feet of Jesus. Others have been wounded in the battles of life, but the tenderness of divine mercy became evident in the restoring power of God's care. John gave excellent advice to his friends when he wrote, "My little children, these things write I unto you, that ye sin not. And if any man sin, we have an advocate with the Father, Jesus Christ the righteous" (1 John 2:1). We cannot walk and stand still at the same moment. If we walk in the light, we walk with God and cannot be alone. To walk with the Lord leads to continual cleansing.

Through His Blood . . . *Paradise is Reached* (Revelation 7:14)

John was surely entranced when God revealed to him the book of Revelation. He saw a great company of people arrayed in white garments and listened as an elder asked, "What are these who are arrayed in white robes? and whence came they?" John replied, "Sir, thou knowest. And he said unto me, These are they which came out of great tribulation, and have washed their robes and made them white in the blood of the Lamb" (Rev. 7:13–14). These saints had already reached their eternal home; their dreams had come true. They were not hoping to reach heaven; they had arrived. The elder explained these people were eternally safe, not because of their identification with any special religious organization nor the intercession of any trusted clergyman, but because they were in the presence of God and their garments had been cleansed in the blood of God's Son.

(1) *A Sincere Desire.* "They washed their robes." It is necessary for us to accept what God provides. Washing machines may be very efficient, but human hands must place the soiled articles into the appliance. The cleansing of dirty clothing varies in certain countries. Nevertheless, unless people desire cleansing and participate in the process, nothing avails in the successful laundering of their soiled clothing. The same truth applies to the lives of men and women. Unless sinners desire to be clean, even God cannot perform what needs to be done. John, referring to the saints in heaven, said, "*They* washed their robes and made them white in the blood of the Lamb."

(2) *A Safe Detergent.* I have often watched Egyptian women placing their soiled garments into the muddy waters of the river

Nile. In India I was fascinated when the Hindus performed similar chores in the filthy waters of the Ganges. Evidently they were satisfied with their efforts because they had no more efficient way of washing their linen. Within Western countries manufacturers spend enormous sums of money advertising products, and competition is keen. They all claim to have the most effective way of getting clothes as white as snow. It is extremely doubtful whether any machine can justify the claims made by its manufacturer. People are now being told that even the snow becomes polluted when falling through a contaminated atmosphere.

It is refreshing to learn that God's remedy for sinful souls is perfect. He can do what other agencies cannot. His detergent is perfect and is supplied without cost! This was evident when John was informed about the cleansing power of the blood of Christ. Sometimes housewives are disappointed when their best efforts fail to remove annoying stains. When the Lord cleanses souls, even the most resistant blemishes disappear forever.

(3)   *A Scintillating Display.* "And the armies which were in heaven followed him upon white horses, clothed in fine linen, white and clean" (Rev. 19:14). This seems to be one of the attractive characteristics of heaven. Describing the transfiguration of the Lord, Luke said, "And as he prayed, the fashion of his countenance was altered, and his raiment was white and glistening [sparkling]" (Luke 9:29). When Matthew described the appearance of the angel at the tomb of the Lord, he wrote, "His countenance was like lightning and his raiment white as snow" (Matt. 28:3).

John Bunyan, in his thrilling book *Pilgrim's Progress*, describes a man who climbed over a wall to begin his pilgrimage toward the celestial city. He considered it unnecessary to pass through the official entrance gate and never went near the cross. Later he was refused admittance to the city of God. Yet Christian, who had been to Calvary, was given a great welcome. The precious blood of Christ was his passport to God's country; it guaranteed an entrance. Blessed are they whose garments have been made white.

"Whereby are given unto us exceeding great and precious promises: that by these ye might be partakers of the divine nature, having escaped the corruption that is in the world through lust" (2 Peter 1:4).

Recently, as my wife and I sat at a table in a Santa Barbara restaurant, a very attractive waitress approached to ask if we were ready to place an order. She was tall and radiant and evidently anxious to please. The young lady was different from the other employees, and I asked, "Are you a Christian?" She smiled and replied, "Yes, Sir, I am. I have attended church all my life, but last September I entered into a relationship with the Lord, and since that time my life has changed." I shall always remember that young woman who said, "I entered into a relationship with Christ."

Millions of church members profess to have faith in Christ, but unfortunately to some of them, Jesus of Nazareth is only a Person who lived and died centuries ago. Apparently they know little if anything of constant communion with the Lord: hearing His voice, obeying His commands, and enjoying His presence. Knowing Christ is not merely an agreement with religious principles. It is the sharing of His grace which extends through life to embrace eternity.

The word partaker comes from the Greek *koinonia*, which means to share, to become a partner. It was used in the Old Testament to indicate when a man became unclean, when he shared a neighbor's defilement. Interpreting the word *koinoneo*, Dr. Thayer says, "It means to come into common fellowship; to become a sharer; to be made a partner." This becomes increasingly interesting when a study of the New Testament reveals progression from the darkness of sin to the splendor of eternity. The word is used in five challenging Scriptures.

Partakers of His Nature (2 Peter 1:4)

This verse written by Simon Peter provides a window through which may be seen the amazing salvation offered by God to sinful people. The apostle was explicit when he reminded his readers they had "escaped the corruption that is in the world." They had been delivered from the power of sin and had received something never previously possessed. Their conversion had been made possible, not because they had accepted a new doctrine, but because they adored a new Deliverer.

It was never revealed whether or not the disciples were present when Nicodemus interviewed Jesus, but at least they knew what the Lord had said, for John recorded a portion of the Master's message. The ruler of the Jews was an educated clergyman, for otherwise he would not have been *the* teacher of the Jewish people. There is reason to believe he was a profound scholar, a sincere theologian, an honored citizen. Yet in spite of his attainments, he needed more than he had. The Lord said to him, "Marvel not that I said unto thee, Ye must be born again" (John 3:7). Unfortunately, that expression has been brought into disrepute by people whose lives leave much to be desired. Born again Christians are not fanatics whose emotional outbursts discredit their teachings, nor people whose morality becomes offensive. They are sincere, believing, God-honoring people whose personal encounter with Christ revolutionized their lives. That transformation can be seen in their daily conduct. Ideas may be changed by what is heard. A new doctrine can alter a man's thoughts, but personal salvation becomes a reality only when Christ is the center of new life.

Probably Paul was endeavoring to express this when he wrote to the Galatians, "My little children, of whom I travail in birth again until Christ be formed in you" (Gal. 4:19). When the Spirit of God implanted seed within the womb of Mary, a process began which reached its climax nine months later in a stable in Bethlehem. The body of the Lord was carefully developed and ultimately brought into the world to fulfill the mission planned in heaven. His birth was a miracle and so is every true conversion. The divine nature cannot be purchased nor deserved. The greatest university in the world cannot supply it, neither can scientists explain it. As parents transmit life to their offspring, God also imparts His life to sinners. Thus begins the process which will never be completed "Till we all come in the unity of the faith, and of the knowledge of the Son of God, unto a perfect man, unto the measure of the stature of the fullness of Christ" (Eph. 4:13). The waitress in the Santa Barbara restaurant had discovered the difference between being a church member and a child of the living God.

Partakers of His Holy Spirit (Hebrews 6:4)

"For it is impossible for those who were once enlightened, and have tasted of the heavenly gift, and were made partakers of the Holy Ghost, And have tasted the good word of God, and the powers of the world to come, If they should fall away, to renew them again unto repentance; seeing they crucify to themselves the Son of God afresh, and put him to an open shame" (Heb. 6:4).

This has been one of the most controversial verses within the Scripture. Those who do not believe in the eternal security of the believer in Christ quote this statement to support their doctrine that even Christians can fall from grace and be lost. Many people find difficulty in harmonizing this utterance with the words of Christ, "My sheep hear my voice, and I know them, and they follow me: And I give unto them eternal life; *and they shall never perish*, neither shall any man pluck them out of my hand" (John 10:27–28). Nevertheless a careful study of the Bible should remove the problems of interpretation.

The writer to the Hebrews proceeded to say, "But, beloved, we are persuaded better things of you" (Heb. 6:9). The letter was sent to Hebrew Christians of whom was said, "For God is not unrighteous to forget your work and labor of love, which ye have shewed toward his name, in that ye have ministered to the saints, and do minister" (Heb. 6:10). These early believers *had not fallen away*, and consequently, the statement about the impossibility of renewal was not addressed to them. The writer, Paul, or whomsoever he might have been, referred to many Jews who had turned back, as it were, from the gates of the kingdom. They had heard and understood the Gospel, had been mentally enlightened by the power of the Holy Spirit, and to some extent had known the pleasure of association with Christ and His church. Yet, in spite of their proximity to the kingdom of God, they had rejected personal commitment. Their refusal to proceed might have been caused by the destruction of their temple, the interference of legalistic teachers, or the increasing persecution of those who followed the Savior. Like the children of Israel, they had seen the Promised Land and had tasted of its fruit, but their unbelief prevented their entering Canaan.

Even in this twentieth century, many people who actively served the church have become the slaves of lust, and many who preached the gospel are now contaminated by degradation. Their bitter tears of anguish cannot remove the stain from their souls nor relieve the remorse in their troubled hearts. Whether or not they were ever truly saved is open to conjecture, but even if they contemplated the possibility of obtaining God's pardon, they cannot forgive themselves.

184

They know "They have crucified the Son of God, and put Him to an open shame."

If Jews who were near to entering the church of Christ could be "partakers" or sharers with the Holy Spirit, the fellowship enjoyed by those who have become the temples of God is infinitely greater. Writing to the Corinthians, Paul said, "Know ye not that ye are the temple of God, and that the Spirit of God dwelleth in you?" (1 Cor. 3:16). Faith brings eternal life to the believer, but the indwelling Spirit of God guarantees that Christ will be formed within the human soul. To become a partner with God in such an experience is among the greatest privileges ever given to men and women. The same Spirit that moved upon the face of the waters at the creation of the world also moves upon the chaos in unregenerate life and brings to pass that which is pleasing to the Lord. Hannah, the mother of Samuel, said in her prayer of thanksgiving, "He raiseth up the poor out of the dust, and lifteth up the beggar from the dunghill, to set them among princes, and to make them inherit the throne of glory" (1 Sam. 2:8). The psalmist reiterated the same sentiments when he wrote, "He raiseth up the poor out of the dust, and lifteth the needy out of the dunghill" (Ps. 113:7–8). Yet God cannot do this alone; He needs our assistance and for that reason permitted men and women to "partake of His Holy Spirit" and become partners in the greatest enterprise ever conceived in the mind of the Almighty.

Partakers of His Promise (Ephesians 3:6)

"That the Gentiles should be fellowheirs, and of the same body, and partakers of his promise in Christ by the gospel." It is worthy of consideration that Paul did not speak here of the *promises* of God. Even in his generation there were innumerable promises that had been made to Israel, and these affected every facet of life. Writing to the believers in Ephesus, the apostle emphasized that his readers had become "fellowheirs, and of the same body, and partakers of his *promise*," which was fulfilled in Christ and proclaimed through the gospel. That special promise was made by God to Abraham, "In thee shall all families of the earth be blessed" (Gen. 12:3). This had remained a mystery hidden throughout the ages, but Paul became the messenger through whom it would be explained to mankind.

He affirmed in the opening statement of Ephesians 3:9 that his task was "to make all men see what is the fellowship of the mystery." When the apostle wrote to the Colossians, he repeated the message, "Whereof I am made a minister, according to the dispensation of God which is given to me for you, to fulfill the word of God; even the mystery which hath been hid from ages and from generations, but now is made manifest to his saints: To whom God would make known what is the riches of the glory of this mystery among the Gentiles which is Christ in you, the hope of glory" (Col. 1:25–27). The apostle used the word mystery seventeen times in his writings.

"The Greek word translated mystery is *musteerion* which means: 'a hidden or secret thing; something not obvious to the understanding; a hidden purpose or counsel; a secret will'" (Thayer). Paul used the word six times in the epistle to the Ephesians (1:9; 3:3; 3:4; 3:9; 5:32; 6:19) and four times in the letter to the Colossians (1:26; 1:27; 2:2; 4:3). The gospel revealed through Christ was God's special surprise for mankind. He had planned, prepared, preserved, perfected, and presented it. It was the glorious news that He loved everyone and desired to make possible the entry of all nations into His family. Even unlovely, unattractive people were appreciated by the Almighty, and through Christ, the most degraded could lean on the bosom of God. To Jews this was unwelcome; it was a stumbling block. To the Greeks it was foolishness, but to every Christian it was the most wonderful message ever proclaimed. God's revealed mystery made possible the words of the poet who wrote:

> Jesus included me;
> Yes, He included me:
> When the Lord said 'Whosoever,'
> He included me."

(Quoted from the author's book *The Exciting Epistle to the Ephesians*, Kregel Publications, 1989, pp. 136–37.)

Partakers of His Holiness (Hebrews 12:10)

"For they [our earthly fathers] verily for a few days chastened us after their own pleasure; but he [God] for our profit, that we might be partakers of his holiness." Loving fathers would never chasten a child unnecessarily. Their experience enables them to foresee things which might be harmful. Their affection guarantees everything possible will be done to preserve children from danger. The writer to the Hebrews emphasized that if this were true of human fathers, it was even more evident with God's attitude toward His children.

186

The Lord desired that we should share (partake of) His nature, become heirs of His vast possessions, and be worthy to enjoy what He supplied. To share His life is a great privilege; to be the recipient of His gracious promise is even better, but to be holy is something that cannot be surpassed. John wrote, "Beloved, now are we the sons of God, and it doth not yet appear what we shall be: but we know that when he shall appear, we shall be like him; for we shall see him as he is" (1 John 3:2).

Paul wrote, "That with all boldness, as always, so now also, Christ shall be magnified in my body, whether it be by life, or by death. For to me to live is Christ, and to die is gain" (Phil. 1:20–21). "Paul's reference to the magnifying glass is most interesting. . . . A magnifying glass does not actually increase the size of anything: it only seems to do this. Actually the object at which a man may be looking is exactly the same size, but the glass brings it into bold relief, and the watcher is able to see it more clearly. It is not possible to make Christ more wonderful for He is the altogether lovely One, and the chiefest among ten thousand. Yet, if by God's grace we can become magnifying glasses—in perfect alignment with the Master and men—they will be able to see Him more clearly when they look at Him through us. All the details of His superb glory may be brought into delightful relief if we are what we ought to be. Paul had a similar thought in mind when he wrote: 'Ye are living epistles, seen and read of all men.' We read the Scriptures to learn more of Christ. Likewise people read us in order to achieve identical results" (quoted from the author's book *Bible Windows*, Kregel Publications, 1985, p. 106). When Christians magnify their Lord, they are truly partaking of God's holiness.

Partakers of His Glory (1 Peter 5:1)

"The elders which are among you I exhort, who am also an elder, and a witness of the sufferings of Christ, and also a partaker of the glory that shall be revealed." The word glory, which comes from the Greek word *doxa*, was one of Peter's favorite expressions. He used it sixteen times in his epistles (see two examples in 1 Peter 5:4 and 1 Peter 5:10). He mentioned the eternal glory to which Christians are called and indicated that "when the chief Shepherd shall appear, ye shall receive a crown of glory that fadeth not away." Peter also mentioned, "an inheritance incorruptible, and undefiled, and that fadeth not away, reserved in heaven for you" (1 Peter 1:4).

God gave to the apostle a clear view of what lay beyond the grave. He saw and appreciated the splendor of his Lord. Yet it was even more wonderful to know that he, Simon Peter, in spite of his failures, would share the glory of his Master.

Dr. Paul Lee Tan in his wonderful book *The Encyclopedia of 7700 Illustrations* quotes a remarkable story from the American Civil War. He says, "During General Sherman's last campaign in the South, certain changes in commanders were made. General Howard was placed at the head of a special division. Soon after this the war ended, and there was to be a grand review of the army in Washington. The night before the review, General Sherman sent for General Howard and said: 'The political friends of the officer you succeeded are determined that he shall ride at the head of the Corps, and I want you to help me out.' 'It is my command,' said General Howard, 'and I am entitled to ride at its head.' 'Of course you are,' replied General Sherman. 'You led those men through Georgia and the Carolinas: but Howard, you are a Christian, and can stand the disappointment.' 'If you put it on that ground,' replied Howard, 'there is but one answer. Let him ride at the head of the corps.' 'Yes, let him have the honor,' replied Sherman, 'but you will report to me at nine o'clock in the morning, and will ride by my side at the head of the entire army.' General Howard protested, but his commander's orders were positive. So on that day, in the grand review, he had a place of honor at the head of the entire army."

There is no commentator in the world who can exhaust the meaning of sharing or partaking of the glory of Christ. If a text may be lifted from its setting, then it can be said, "Eye hath not seen, nor ear heard, neither have entered into the heart of man, the things which God hath prepared for them that love him" (1 Cor. 2:9). Perhaps Charles H. Gabriel was nearest to the truth when he wrote:

> When all my labors and trials are o'er,
> And I am safe on that beautiful shore,
> Just to be near the dear Lord I adore
> Will through the ages be glory for me.
>
> O that will be glory for me,
> Glory for me, glory for me;
> When by His grace I shall look on His face,
> *That* will be glory, be glory for me.

"And beside this, giving all diligence, add to your faith virtue; and to virtue knowledge; and to knowledge temperance; and to temperance patience; and to patience godliness; And to godliness brotherly kindness; and to brotherly kindness charity. For if these things be in you, and abound, they make you that ye shall neither be barren nor unfruitful in the knowledge of our Lord Jesus Christ" (2 Peter 1:5–8).

People who have no hobby often become bored with their existence. They have no enthusiasm about anything and never appreciate the zest for living. Individuals who collect stamps, rocks, and coins are always seeking new specimens for their collections. As an adult I became interested in seashells and searched everywhere for new and valuable species. The late King Farouk of Egypt had a large collection of matchboxes, and many wealthy people have a love for antiques and art. I have friends who collect ceramic forms of owls and snails, and others who exhibit interest in all kinds of collectibles. I knew a man in South Africa who collected cats; he had a hundred, and I always wondered how the neighbors tolerated the miniature zoo that existed on the other side of the garden fence. The apostle Peter was interested in a different kind of collectible. He valued spiritual realities and urged his readers to increase what they already possessed. He wrote, "And beside this, *add* to your faith, virtue . . . knowledge . . . temperance . . . patience." The fact that he encouraged his friends *to add* these things, suggested they did not already possess them; their collections were incomplete.

Faith

This is the beginning of any spiritual collection, for without it we have nothing. There are degrees of faith, for the Savior spoke of *no faith* (see Mark 4:37–40); *little faith* (see Matt. 6:25–30); and *great faith* (see Luke 7:1–10). Without true faith in Christ people remain dead in trespasses and sins, and lifeless people do not collect anything. Peter, introducing his letter, said, "Simon Peter, a servant and an apostle of Jesus Christ, to them that have obtained like precious faith, through the righteousness of God and our Savior Jesus Christ" (2 Peter 1:1). His readers had been indifferent until the grace of God transformed them. Then, they "obtained like precious faith." Peter's converts acquired something not previously possessed. Their experience was not the result of an emotional upheaval, nor something obtained through self-effort. They had been changed by the kindness and mercy of God, taken the first step in Christian experience, and received their first jewel. The apostle, who was a man of great knowledge, urged them to seek other treasures in order to increase their collection.

Virtue

The new relationship with Christ transformed their conduct; their actions should reflect the teachings they had embraced. Virtue would express inner serenity, the fruit produced by the indwelling Spirit of God. Faith without virtue would be meaningless. Paul mentioned Hymenaeus and Alexander, whose confession apparently was only an intellectual idea (see 1 Tim. 1:19–20). Doctrines that do not produce virtue are stillborn!

It is noteworthy in regard to these collectibles, Peter on five different occasions mentioned "these things" (see 1 Peter 1:8–10, 12, 15). The apostle believed that a barren life would be as unattractive as the fig tree that disappointed Christ (see Matt. 21:19). When the Lord spoke of the vine, He outlined three stages of fruitbearing: fruit, more fruit, and much fruit (see John 15:1–5). *Webster's New International Dictionary* describes virtue as "a specific excellence; any good quality or merit; excellence in general." The Savior was the embodiment of virtue, and therefore it may be assumed that faith in Christ will increase likeness to Him.

Knowledge

Wisdom is never superlative except in God. It is an unexplored area of understanding. Fellowship with Christ promotes an intense yearning to know more about Him. Knowledge is a rare collectible which, unfortunately, is not possessed by everybody. There are two areas where this treasure may be sought.

(1) *The Written Word of God.* The Scriptures supply everything needed for victorious living. The Bible reveals many invaluable truths, but the greatest is the revelation that Jesus, the Son of God, came into the world to redeem sinners. It is essential that everybody should know more about Him. Yet, however wonderful that knowledge may be, to know Christ personally is even more desirable.

(2) *The Living Word of God.* Paul was devoted to the cause of Christ, and his knowledge of the Savior was unsurpassed, but as a mature saint, he wrote: "Yea doubtless, and I count all things but

190

loss for the excellency of the knowledge of Christ Jesus my Lord: for whom I have suffered the loss of all things, and do count them but dung, that I may win Christ . . . *that I may know him*, and the power of his resurrection, and the fellowship of his sufferings, being made conformable unto his death" (Phil. 3:8–10). There is a great difference between knowing about the Queen of England and being her personal friend. The same truth applies to a relationship with the King of Kings. Knowledge is a treasure of incalculable worth.

Temperance or Self-Control

Faith, virtue, and knowledge point to God, but patience indicates attention is being directed to human conduct. The desire to please God is one thing; to do so is another. The human sanctuary is not always as clean as it should be, and there are occasions when alien residents reside within the holy place (see Neh. 13:6–7). When Jesus went into the temple of God, He saw pollution, greed, and thieves, and He expelled the offenders. He said, "It is written, My house shall be called a house of prayer; but ye have made it a den of thieves" (see Matt. 21:13). The money changers never voluntarily left their tables. To maintain the sanctity of the human soul, resolution and determination are required to put aside "all guile, and hypocrisies, and envies, and all evil speakings" (1 Peter 2:1). As discipline is found in the life of a soldier, so self-control and temperance must be evident as a Christian struggles against evil.

Patience

This is one of the most desired gems in any spiritual collection. It involves trust and is best seen in Job, whose patience was severely tested in the problems that devastated his life. The patriarch endured until he emerged victoriously. The writer to the Hebrews urged his friends to "run with patience the race that is set before us" (Heb. 12:1). It is relatively easy to maintain trust when circumstances are favorable, but the task becomes difficult when life is overwhelmed by failure and frustration. When God seems reluctant or slow to answer prayers, faith is challenged, and people become weary and despondent. Job said: "He knoweth the way that I take: when he hath tried me, I shall come forth as gold" (Job 23:10). Rare collectibles are often discovered in unlikely places.

Godliness

For several years I was an avid collector of seashells and possessed thousands of specimens of all colors, shapes, and sizes. I knew their Latin names, the location and depth of water in which they were found, and my search for special treasures was ceaseless. I regularly sent parcels to overseas collectors, and there were occasions when I either found or received new gems. A lady with whom I often exchanged specimens sent me a special shell which at that time was one of six in the world. I proudly displayed that specimen in my cabinet. Similarly, when Peter mentioned *godliness*, he referred to a rare commodity, a treasure not often found in the lives of men and women. To see it in radiant Christians is an experience not easily forgotten. My friend Mr. Bottomley who lived in Melbourne, Australia, was asked by a little girl, "Mr. Bot, are you God?" He replied, "No, sweetheart, but I'm trying to be like Him." Rare gems are not obtained easily.

Brotherly Kindness

Some of the most valuable items in any collection are not beautiful, and some of the attractive specimens are not rare. The list of collectibles supplied by Simon Peter illustrates that fact. It is a saddening fact that the media thrives on unpleasant stories. If a citizen does something bad, denunciations are printed and circulated. If a man does a special act of kindness, little if anything is ever mentioned. People take things for granted and often forget to return thanks for help received. The Savior came to earth to help everybody, and Christians should emulate His example. It has often been said, "Actions speak louder than words, and one kind deed may be worth a hundred sermons." The first act of the church after Pentecost was the formation of an administration capable of feeding the hungry and giving shelter to the homeless. John expressed the doctrines of the church when he wrote, "But whoso hath this world's good, and seeth his brother have need, and shutteth up his bowels of compassion from him, how dwelleth the love of God in him?" (1 John 3:17).

Within the early church donors gave of their possessions and never asked if recipients deserved a gift. They gave without question, and great grace was upon the assemblies. Simon Peter lived in a world dominated by Roman greed where many victims became like their conquerors. The soldiers took whatever they desired; selfishness dictated their conduct. When the followers of Jesus sacrificed to assist less fortunate brethren, the world saw moral excellence that was rare. Nothing can be more admirable than affection that embraces all people. If that were practiced internationally, wars would cease immediately. A helping hand is better than advice; kindness is more to be desired than orations. Peter urged his readers to *add* this to their collection.

Charity ... *Love*

The thirteenth chapter of the first letter sent by Paul to the Corinthians is probably one of the best-known parts of the New Testament. There the apostle endeavored to explain the reality of Christian affection. He reached a glorious climax when he wrote, "And now abideth faith, hope, charity, these three; but the greatest of these is charity" (1 Cor. 13:13). Life and language have two extremes. Vocabularies mention murder, vice, cruelty, envy, malice, bitterness, greed, jealousy, strife, and bloodshed. People who exhibit such characteristics are never popular. As a contrast, there are gentleness, kindness, goodness, sympathy, charm, beauty, affection, assistance, and grace. All who possess these attributes are admired people.

Love is not jealous of a rival's prosperity and never broadcasts news of another's failure or disgrace. It hides what threatens a good reputation. Love seeks ways to assist and asks nothing in return. It pardons but never pouts; it beautifies but never besmirches. True love emanates from God, for He is love. Peter urged his readers to add it to their spiritual collections. Earthly treasures are either sold or bequeathed to relatives or friends. The jewels mentioned by Peter enrich their owners through time and into eternity. If men are willing to spend enormous sums of money to increase their perishable assets, Christians should heed Peter's advice to acquire spiritual gems. The psalmist said, "For when he dieth, he shall carry nothing away" (Ps. 49:17). The Savior was very wise when He said, "Lay not up for yourselves treasures upon earth, where moth and rust doth corrupt, and where thieves break through and steal: But lay up for yourselves treasures in heaven, where neither moth nor rust doth corrupt, and where thieves do not break through nor steal: For where your treasure is, there will your heart be also" (Matt. 6:19–21).

"But grow in grace, and in the knowledge of our Lord and Savior Jesus Christ" (2 Peter 3:18).

Ambition is one of the most compelling forces in existence. Webster's Dictionary defines it as "An eager and sometimes inordinate desire for something, as preferment, honor, superiority, power, fame, wealth, etc. The desire to distinguish oneself in some way." It is the motivating force which ignores failure, overcomes weakness, and persists until a desired goal is reached. Ask an athlete about his ambition and he will probably express a desire to become the greatest in his profession. A politician wistfully dreams of becoming the president of his country. A young bank clerk may wish to become a successful financier. A medical student may want to become a famous surgeon with his own hospital. An old Christian was asked about his greatest desire, and after reflection, he replied, "I have three great yearnings: *to be found in Christ, to be like Christ,* and *to be with Christ.*" Had he given greater consideration to the question, he might have added three others, for the Bible reveals six steps that lead to a golden throne.

Desiring Christ . . . Sincerity . . . *An Undeniable Plea*

"And there were certain Greeks among them that came up to worship at the feast: The same came therefore to Philip, which was of Bethsaida of Galilee, and desired him, saying, Sir, we would see Jesus" (John 12:20–21). Nothing of spiritual value can be done for anyone until he becomes aware of his need to meet Christ. God may supply a banquet, but if the guests refuse to eat what has been supplied, nothing more can be done. The Savior walked through the streets of Jericho, but if the blind beggar had remained silent, he would not have received sight. Multitudes of people attended the feast at Jerusalem, and many might have been interested in meeting Christ. The Greeks did not walk aimlessly around the streets; they found a man who could introduce them to Jesus and asked for assistance. God said, "I love them that love me; and those that seek me early shall find me" (Prov. 8:17). Solomon realized that knowing God was of paramount importance; it was not something to be postponed until a more convenient time. To find the Lord should be man's greatest desire. The Greeks who came to Jerusalem were consumed with a passionate longing to meet the Man from Galilee, and their eyes shone with pleasure when their dreams were fulfilled. The prospectors who panned for gold in the mountain streams of California seldom abandoned their search for the precious metal. When seekers after Christ exhibit that kind of determination, they succeed. David said, "Blessed are they . . . that seek him with *the whole heart*" (Ps. 119:2).

In Christ . . . Salvation . . . *A Unique Position*

"Therefore if any man be *in Christ*, he is a new creature: old things are passed away; behold, all things are become new" (2 Cor. 5:17). It is important to know that men may be attracted to Christ, may listen to His Word and even admire Him, and yet not be His disciples. To belong to a listening audience is one thing, to worship at His feet is another.

The term "in Christ" was one of Paul's favorite expressions. The apostle probably seldom, if ever, asked to what church a believer belonged. He taught that fellowship with other Christians was desirable and spent the greater part of his life establishing assemblies where Christians could worship together. Yet, when he referred to his associates, he said they were "*in Christ.*" For example, he spoke of "Andronicus and Junia, my kinsmen, and my fellow prisoners, who are of note among the apostles, who also *were in Christ before me*" (Rom. 16:7). The same statement or definition appears in several places throughout his epistles. To be "in Christ" means that His presence and power encircle the saint. Something has happened. Those who were outside are now inside! It speaks of identification. Men and women have entered into His grace and fellowship.

Sheep that are within the fold of the shepherd can depend upon his care; they each belong to the other. To be "in Christ" means acceptance by Him; He is pleased to be associated with us. When Adam accepted and put on the garment of skins which God supplied in the garden of Eden, human nakedness was covered. When believers put on the garments of salvation (see Isa. 61:10), God sees not their insufficiency, but the righteousness of Christ by which they are clothed. To be "in Christ" means that God has accepted them as His children. His love overshadows their sin; His grace removes their shame. They are *in Christ*, and that is a unique position. It is not known whether the Greeks who sought to see Jesus ever reached this stage on the royal highway to heaven, but for those who love and serve Him, Christ said, "My sheep hear my voice, and I know them, and they follow me: And I give unto them eternal life; and they shall never perish, neither shall any man pluck them out of my hand" (John 10:27–28).

For Christ . . . Service . . . *An Unashamed Profession*

"And John answered and said, Master, we saw one casting out devils in thy name; and we forbad him, because he followeth not with us. And Jesus said unto him, Forbid him not: for he that is not against us is *for us*" (Luke 9:49–50). It would be interesting to know more about the mysterious man who was rebuked by the Lord's disciples. Evidently he had heard the Savior and his life had been influenced by the power of God. He apparently left his occupation to become an evangelist. For undisclosed reasons the new preacher chose not to be identified with the apostles. He decided to be independent, and his activities caused concern among the disciples. Whether John became jealous of the stranger's success or shocked by his independence is not known. The apostle and his colleagues watched the man's exploits but disliked the fact that he did not belong to their company. He was a stranger who had never been commissioned to evangelize the villages. They urged him to cease preaching, but it is doubtful that he obeyed their instructions.

Modern critics would say he did not belong to the authorized convention! He should remain silent, for the elders' hands had not been placed upon his head! This was the first appearance of denominational superiority among the followers of Jesus. Unfortunately, it was not the last. The man was definitely casting out devils; therefore it must be concluded he was a genuine exorcist. His success was achieved through his faith in the name of Jesus. It is difficult to believe he was trying to increase his popularity or that he suffered from an inflated ego. Had his motives for service been insincere, the demons would have exposed his hypocrisy (compare Acts 19:13–16).

Jesus was not surprised by John's announcement. He said, "He that is not against us, is *for us*." The Lord is far more important than any group of believers who claim to be associated with Him. Unfortunately, prejudice has made it difficult for some people to discern that fact. When we love the Lord, we serve—any other course of action would be unpardonable.

Through Christ . . . Success . . . *An Unlimited Power*

"I know both how to be abased, and I know how to abound; every where and in all things I am instructed both to be full and to be hungry, both to abound and to suffer need. I can do all things *through Christ* which strengtheneth me" (Phil. 4:12–13). No person did more for the extension of Christ's kingdom than Paul. Within his lifetime he evangelized the world of his day, he continued his work in spite of great hazards, and finally, when he reached journey's end, he said, "For I am now ready to be offered, and the time of my departure is at hand. I have fought a good fight, I have finished my course, I have kept the faith: henceforth there is laid up for me a crown of righteousness" (2 Tim. 4:6–8). Paul desired others to know that victory came *through Christ;* it was not the result of self-effort, nor because he was too proud to admit defeat.

The story of Paul's amazing exploits provides exciting reading, for he triumphed where other men would have failed. He was an untiring missionary who continued his work until he was killed in Rome. He refused to quit. When difficulties loomed as mountains ahead, he either climbed or went around them, but he never turned back. He had placed his hand to the plow and was determined to complete his God-given task. The reason for his success was explained clearly in his epistles. He believed the risen Lord lived in the souls of all who had become temples of the Holy Spirit. Writing to the church in Corinth, he said, "Know ye not that ye are the temple of God, and that the Spirit of God dwelleth you?" (1 Cor. 3:16).

Paul believed that when he was united with God's Holy Spirit, no difficulty was insurmountable and no problem insoluble. Occasionally, as in the prison in Jerusalem, he became despondent, but even there the Lord renewed the promise that Paul would preach before Caesar (see Acts 23:11). Together they faced every trial, shared each emotion. When Paul sent his message to the church in Philippi, he emphasized that everything was possible through Christ—who was present with him. Christians should never forget this important fact.

Like Christ . . . Sanctification . . . *An Unspoiled Purity*

"He that saith he abideth in him ought himself so to walk, even as he walked" (1 John 2:6). "Beloved, now are we the sons of God, and it doth not yet appear what we shall be: but we know that, when he shall appear, we shall be *like him;* for we shall see him as he is" (1 John 3:2).

The followers of Christ were first called disciples. The word, or name, was a translation of *matheetes* which meant a pupil or stu-

197

dent. Eminent philosophers walked through the countryside, teaching as they went. Their students accompanied them and listened to the lesson as it was given. Similarly, the disciples of Jesus followed Him and learned as they walked. Evidently they were attentive scholars, for the words of the Savior were reproduced in the Gospels. John and his colleagues were called disciples. With the passing of time that word became unsatisfactory. The listeners had become like their Teacher! This was recognized in the city of Antioch. Luke wrote, "And the disciples were called Christians first in Antioch" (Acts 11:26).

As the church grew in grace and size, watching citizens recognized the members were different from their unconverted neighbors. They lived according to standards of morality undesired by other people. John expressed that fact when he wrote, "He that saith he abideth in him [Christ] ought himself also so to walk, even as he walked" (1 John 2:6). Paul expressed a similar truth when he wrote of growing from a child to become a mature adult, of desiring the meat of the word instead of milk (see Eph. 4:15; 1 Cor. 3:2). Every Christian should earnestly strive to be like Christ. That goal will ultimately be reached, for John wrote, "Beloved, now are we the sons of God, and it doth not yet appear what we shall be: but we know that, when he shall appear, *we shall be like him*; for we shall see him as he is" (1 John 3:2).

The most effective advertisement for Christ is a dedicated, sanctified life. The Holy Spirit was sent to the church to transform sinners into saints. That He succeeded in Antioch became evident, for the citizens of that city believed the name "disciples" did not reflect the character of the people in their midst. The followers of Christ had become like their Lord—they were all little Christs!—they were Christians. Any believer who has no ambition to emulate that example is an enigma.

With Christ . . . Serenity . . . *An Unceasing Pleasure*

The intensity of Paul's love for Christ may be detected in his statement to the church at Philippi. He wrote, "For I am in a strait betwixt two, having a desire to depart, and to be *with Christ*; which is far better: Nevertheless to abide in the flesh is more needful for you" (Phil. 1:23–24). In spite of blemishes this world is a place no one wishes to leave—unless continuing pain has made existence unbearable. No person wants to die—unless something has destroyed the desire to live. Paul was a notable exception to that rule. His reasons for wanting to live and continue his service for Christ were unmistakable. Yet when he contrasted the pleasure of serving Christ on earth and abiding in His presence in heaven, the apostle knew which was more desirable. He could not imagine anything that would supersede the thrill of seeing his Lord and remaining in His presence forever. That was the ultimate joy.

Writing to the Thessalonians, Paul said, "For the Lord himself shall descend from heaven with a shout with the voice of the archangel, and with the trump of God: and the dead in Christ shall rise first: Then we which are alive and remain shall be caught up together with them in the clouds, to meet the Lord in the air: and so shall we ever be *with the Lord*. Wherefore comfort one another with these words" (1 Thess. 4:16–18).

> Some day my earthly house will fall,
> I cannot tell how soon 'twill be;
> But this I know—my All in All
> Has now a place in heav'n for me.
>
> And I shall see Him face to face,
> And tell the story—Saved by grace.

SCRIPTURE TEXT INDEX

203

204

BIBLIOGRAPHY

Amplified New Testament. Grand Rapids: Zondervan Publishing House, 1958.

Barclay, W. *The Gospel of Mark.* Philadelphia: Westminster Press, 1954.

Cowman, Mrs. Charles. *Streams in the Desert.* Los Angeles: Cowman Publishing Company, 1960.

Englishman's Greek Testament. London: Samuel Baxter and Company, 1877.

Funk and Wagnall's Encyclopedia. New York: Standard Reference Works Publishers.

Josephus, Flavius. *The Complete Works of Josephus.* Grand Rapids: Kregel Publications, 1960.

Powell, Ivor. *Mark's Superb Gospel.* Grand Rapids: Kregel Publications, 1985.

Powell, Ivor. *John's Wonderful Gospel.* Grand Rapids: Kregel Publications, 1983.

Powell, Ivor. *The Exciting Ephesians.* Grand Rapids: Kregel Publications, 1989.

Powell, Ivor. *Bible Gems.* Grand Rapids: Kregel Publications, 1987.

Powell, Ivor. *Bible Windows.* Grand Rapids: Kregel Publications, 1985.

Tan, P. L. *Encyclopedia of 7,700 Illustrations.* Rockville: Assurance Publishers, 1979.

Thayer, J. H. *Greek-English Lexicon.* Edinburgh: T & T Clark, 1901.

Thompson, W. M. *The Land and the Book.* New York: Thomas Nelson and Sons, 1910.

The Zondervan Pictorial Encyclopedia. Grand Rapids: Zondervan Publishing House, 1975.